St. Joseph Has Lost His Hammer:

How Bullying and Hazing Has Swamped Our Nation's Schools and How Best to Stop It.

Dominic M. Martin

St. Joseph Has Lost His Hammer:

How Bullying and Hazing Has Swamped Our Nation's Schools and How Best to Stop It.

Dominic M. Martin

iUniverse, Inc.
Bloomington

St. Joseph Has Lost His Hammer:
How Bullying and Hazing Has Swamped Our
Nation's Schools and How Best to Stop It.

iUniverse books may be ordered through booksellers or by contacting:

iUniverse
1663 Liberty Drive
Bloomington, IN 47403
www.iuniverse.com
1-800-Authors (1-800-288-4677)

ISBN: 978-1-4620-3281-5 (sc)
ISBN: 978-1-4620-3482-6 (ebk)

Printed in the United States of America

iUniverse rev. date: 07/28/2011

CONTENTS

Chapter One: Raven.. 1

Chapter Two: Rough and Ready.................................. 24

Chapter Three: Rule the Roast 141

The Epistle of Paul to Titus

The grace of God has appeared, offering salvation to all men. It trains us to reject godless ways and worldly desires, and live temperately, justly, and devoutly in this age as we await our blessed hope, the appearing of the glory of the great God and of our Savior Christ Jesus. It was he who sacrifices himself for us, to redeem us from all unrighteousness and to cleanse for himself a people of his own, eager to do what is right.

New American Bible; Catholic Book Publishing Co: New York, NY, 1970. Chapter 2, Verse 11-14

Author's Note

The four of us, the parents, Catherine and Dominic, and, the children, Emily and Edward, are descended happily from Celtic stock, the better to fight injustice. Indeed, the father's mother was a MacFarlane, one whose motto seen below, states: "This I'll defend." During this battle about which you are about to read, the parents often thought of that combative phrase and, too, the prickly thistle–the Scottish sign of defiance–when defending their children. Now, they know that they were both too late and too slow in that defense, a mistake which will never again be repeated.

The three chapters:

      1) Raven
      2) Rough and Ready
      3) Rule the Roast

are designed to conjure the proverbial three R's:

      1) Reading
      2) Writing
      3) Arithmetic,

sometimes written as:

      1) Readin'
      2) 'Rightin'
      3) 'Rithmetic,

That triumvirate is meant to summarize the 3 central aspects of a proper education: What does it mean now to be educated? Ask. Task. Since one needs to build a book like a chubby baker bakes a German chocolate cake, full of coconut: One layer at a time.

Chapter One: Raven

Raven: A bird of ill omen; fabled to forebode death, and to bring infection and bad luck.

> "The raven himself is hoarse
> That croaks the fatal entrance of Duncan
> Under my battlements."
>> William Shakespeare.
>> Macbeth. I.V.39.
> From <u>Brewer's</u> <u>Dictionary</u> <u>of</u> <u>Phrase</u> <u>and</u> <u>Fable</u>
> (Cassell Publishers Ltd. London, 1988 p. 927)

The word "raven" was chosen because, after seeing what my wife and I have seen in the last three years, we believe that our public schools are sick and failing and that, therefore, our society and culture are dying. As my cousin, Jim Garvey says: "Public school education is more than a waste of time. It is a detriment."

Here we go!

In the fall of 2007, when our oldest daughter enrolled in the local high school as a sophomore, I held no expectation that, within weeks, she would be called "a slut" by some of her classmates. I had no premonition that she would be involved in a fist fight not ten weeks later during her first course of the day, an incident requiring a hospital visit since her shoulder had been bruised. At the same time, furthest from my head was the idea that within days some of her classmates would leave scores of vicious, scurrilous, and pornographic voice mails and text messages on her cell phone. And on and on.

It is clear now, looking back as one does, that I had made a series of inaccurate assumptions. I had assumed that civility, engendered by a constant, firm, discipline, would reign. And, in turn, I had held that incorrect thought because well-nigh forty-five years ago, ("Don't say it, sir; don't say it since I know it can't be true! Ha!") when I had entered high school, any form of bad behavior, any sort of discourtesy, any diminution from a steady discipline would not have been tolerated. The miscreant would have been instantly sacked. The mischief-maker would not have been asked back. The malefactor, immediately, would have been shown the door by Fr. Patrick X. Nidorf, the nearly giddy prefect of discipline. Surely, all freshman, including myself, feared him. For, he relished his job, as a child relishes candy. He, it seemed, actually <u>looked</u> <u>forward</u> to kicking naughty, rebellious students out of the school.

It, Villanova Preparatory School, in Ojai, California, was famous for its strict discipline. On those days when Fr. Nidorf expelled multiple students, and they were many, he seemed to walk, or so I then thought and now recall, with a special, almost gleeful, bounce to his step. Many new students would then arrive to replace those turned out, and most of them, I am sure, anticipated neither the stark discipline with which they would be met nor the heavy and unalterable academic load of coursework that they would be required to complete. Many did not measure up and were soon dismissed; some, I am sure, complained, mightily to their parents and were allowed to leave, seeking softer environments. So frantic was the coming-and-going, of students from all over the globe, Mexico, Japan, Iran, Honduras, arriving and leaving, arriving and leaving, that often seemed to me, as I dozed or dreamt on early morning bus rides, interminable and bumpy, returning from some distant game wherein we had gotten ourselves handily slaughtered, often, I conjured, the school had become in this most stubborn of dreams, not a school but a giant department store, one with an enormous revolving door at its front, a turnstile as large as the store itself, a door which never stopped nor slowed, one full of faces coming and going, arriving and leaving, either happy or sad or, sometimes, hesitant and fearful. As I awoke, I asked: "Was my face there among them?"

And now, as I look backwards deep into the past, through the decades of time elapsed, as any father might who wishes to understand what is happening to his daughter or son, and why, and how, I task myself with the simplest of questions: What has changed so fundamentally in our schools? Why? And, finally, asking that one word of question which is always the most difficult one to answer: How?

At some point back in time and let us say, for purposes of brevity, that it was one score ago, under the mistaken aegis of the various too-powerful teacher's unions, new and unwarranted rights were granted to students. Chief among them: They could not be corporally punished. They could not be intimidated or made fearful. They had to be treated as adults, more or less, that is, always reasonably. Any hand may not be laid upon them. Thus, overnight, their wishes, desires, and prerogatives became predominate. All discipline metered out had to be proportionate and strictly non-physical. In short, the ancient dictum from Proverbs (Chapter 13, Verse 24): "He who spares his rod hates his son; but he that loves him takes care to chastise him," was abandoned or cast aside. All of a sudden, the students had a whole new slew of rights, rights of all sorts of measure and form, some so large as to be uncalculable.

Simultaneously, of course, the teachers received an ipso facto pay raise, that is, if one assumes, beforehand, that 20% of a teacher's job had been to parcel out discipline. Now, with these new and expanding strictures on what was suitable for a teacher to do, there was so much less disciplinary work to carry out. At that instant of the changeover, from the old and strict regime to the new and flexible one, might it not have been proper or fortuitous to cut teacher's pay by that same 20%? I fear that nobody asked the question.

This granting of brand new rights to the students across the country happened at the same point as new rights were given to so many others, the wheelchair-bound, regular employees and charges, (especially those in the public sector), and, a little later, to gays. Suddenly, or so it then seemed, nearly everyone and all sorts of groups were clamoring for more rights. What about the rights of children with peanut allergies to not be exposed to peanut-laden air? What about the rights of Sulphur Dioxide-sensitive adults to know whether a certain wine contains sulfites? What about the right of a coffee drinker to be informed that a cup of coffee was hot, at least to some commercial standard? And what about the right, a little later, of a gay-leaning teen to not have his later or possible choice in sexuality derided in the classroom? Rights, rights; they all came marching in, in droves, droves.

Certainly, then, discipline was relaxed; but, then again, that word may be too soft. Perhaps, I should say, "Truncated," or "Made lax or loose." Any reasonable person (whom I do not claim to be) will ask: "Why did this disciplinary diminution take place?" I believe that the answer is fairly obvious: The decline in discipline matches in time our society's embrace of Moral Relativism, that uncertain mantra of most progressives (if that is the correct word), those who perhaps have eschewed God and His Ten Commandment in favor of a less obedient passage through life. At the same time, roughly, that we said "God is Dead," or "Do your own thing," we made passive and weak a school's authority, apparently thinking, poorly, that nothing disastrous would ever happen. This was an experiment, a never-before-tried test. Now, all over our nation, we see the harmful consequences of these decisions: Bullying and hazing are nearly everywhere, test scores are, if not abysmal, quite poor, and the school dropout rates remain obdurately fixed at approximately 25% regardless of state, a fact that makes the true cost of education per year go from spendthrift $15,000 to a scandalous $20,000. This last idea is the unhealthy, i.e., non-white elephant in the room that nobody high up in the teaching profession wishes to discuss.

By the way, there is no reason to assume that spending more money on education works. Those in charge always imply the following:

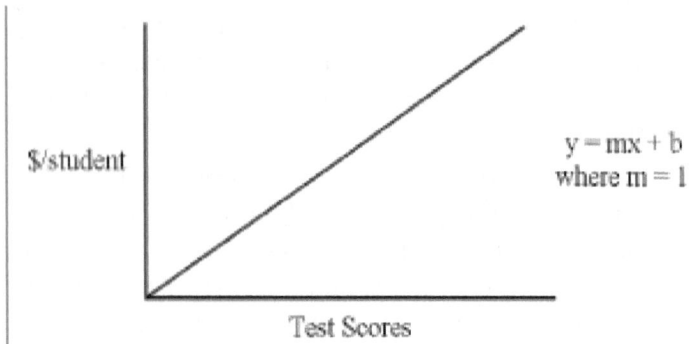

$y = mx + b$
where $m = 1$

\$/student

Test Scores

The reality, however, is this:

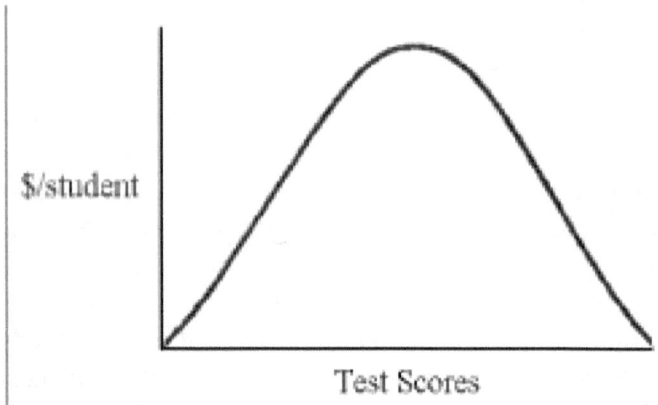

\$/student

Test Scores

That is to say, at some point optimal spending exists, and beyond it, further spending is actually counter-production. Today, school officials do not want to acknowledge this idea. Funny: Years ago I sent this discussion and these two graphs to the Superintendent of Education for Chittenden County in Vermont and I never heard back from her.

Let us return more directly to the bullying and hazing question: Why do we treat those 13 to 18 year olds as adults? Aren't they, in fact, teenagers with incomplete brains, raging hormones, unstable emotional spheres, still growing femurs and ulnae? Why would we ever expect adult behavior from near-kids? Is this not inherently problematic? Is it not foolish to expect maturities, balanced viewpoints, mature magnanimities, controlled emotions, guarded behaviors, etc. from teenagers? Why are we surprised when students do not act carefully? Aren't the teen years normally fraught with the keenest biologic difficulties, including but not limited to acne's incipiency and libido's raging onslaught? And is that not why the "old rules" were put in place in the first instance, to guard and protect and quell the renegade student? Why would school leaders not naturally assume that most teenagers crave to snap bra straps, to cuss, to brag, to race cars, and to swill any form of alcohol? I fear naiveté is not the answer to all these similar questions. No, I believe some students, 20 years ago, egged on by the always "rights-conscious" American Civil Liberties Union (ACLU) clamored, stupidly, for more rights and school leaders, even more stupidly, greatly acceded to those demands, perhaps not realizing the greater and unforeseen consequence of that action: That, thenceforth, authority would be fundamentally undercut and that consequently, in many schools, a fundamental respect for teachers, almost a palpable fear, would disappear, and, finally, that it would be the students, not the teachers, who basically would run the show.

Thus, authority is nowhere near the strong abiding force it once was. Many students openly mock the castrated male teacher who knows, upon fear of dismissal, that he can raise neither a hand no a loud voice against a student. Since they know that reprisals are slim, many students flaunt the rules, especially with regard to dress codes and cell phone usage. Here, I must insert a brief caveat. This story is mostly about the, say 10% constituting the bad kids (or the good kids doing bad things which amounts to the same thing). How does one handle the disruptive teenager, the kid who does not want to learn? Most students are curious, wanting to learn in an atmosphere congenial and fearless, and these youths, by far the majority, clearly need less discipline than the unruly and belligerent ones.

A central question occurs at this juncture. How does a teacher, faced with a bad kid who has done something wrong, or, indeed, a good kid who has done something egregious, how does that teacher compel obedience? George Washington once said, "All life is force." Yet, today, with such corroded authority, with such weakened and sloppy discipline, where is the required, exacting force? Where is the constraining impulse? It used to be that a teacher could use mild physical force or verbal intimidation to sustain a disciplined atmosphere in the classroom; however, now, ironically, he can only ask the student to behave, that is, of course, after the student has already done something incorrect. We are asking that teacher to teach, but we have taken many of the tools that he needs to properly perform that task away from him.

That is how and why I thought of St. Joseph, the carpenter and father of Jesus. Let us say that years ago he is meant to build a house for Jesus and Mary, yet he is told (by the ACLU? By Herod?) that in its construction he may never use a hammer. Would not that stricture make the job, automatically, nearly impossible? That is why I call this small book: St. Joseph Has Los His Hammer. I hope that he does not mind my using his name to make my point. The teachers and St. Joseph, according to this brief fantasy, have the same problems: They both lack the tools to do the job correctly. Without an atmosphere of discipline, without some small smoldering fear, without the suggestion of intimidation, some students will "act out," feeling that they are equal or superior to their teachers. Consequently, some students will tell the teachers what to do, instead of the other way around.

In this discussion of how the teachers have abdicated their responsibility to teach in a controlled and civil setting, one must first turn to Peter Brimelow's incisive book: The Worm in the Apple: How the Teachers' Unions Are Destroying American Education. (Harper Collins; New York; 2003). That book searingly, stunningly charts the decline of our nation's schools, and, concomitantly, the volcanic rise of teacher union power and the equally Herculean increase in school spending. Brimelow punctures the teacher-engendered myth that small class size is essential for learning. (Eighty-three rampaging eager beavers filled the classroom of my first grade class; the time was September, 1957. Only a month later, on October 4, 1957, the Russians would launch Sputnik, thereby confirming their technological superiority, at least for a time, before we "buckled down" as my father used to say.) Brimelow describes the pitiful test scores emanating from most of our school, the decrease, gradual and corrosive, of general knowledge, and the decline of intellectual vigor and curiosity. Further, he shows how the teachers' unions, through their powerful lobbying arms (like the tentacles of a 3-headed, 8-limbed octopus enwrapping itself around a hopeless prey), through large cash donations to thereby tainted legislators, have influenced corruptly laws that only stand to benefit teachers. Collusion's feted air fills the halls of all of our state capitals. Brimelow details how these unfunded state mandates are putting a terrible cash squeeze upon financially hapless communities, which must comply with these dishonest laws though they did not pass them, and which can only raise property taxes to venal and un-American levels to pay their bills. Finally, he delineates the out-of-control spending, including salaries, health benefits and pensions, that marks public schools over the last twenty years. So convincing, so damning is his case that after finishing each chapter I had to fling it down upon a soft sofa to quell my mounting rage. Brimelow makes me think that today's teachers are like the automakers of the 70's: Asking for far too much and doing far too little, and in the process, of course, killing the golden goose. Clearly, heroically, his book sounds a clarion call for reform of our nation's school; yet, little has taken place since its publication seven years ago, and that pathetic inaction is most disturbing to me. I wanted to mention his excellent book early on since it is so pertinent to so many aspects of this discussion.

But, let us return to the heart of the matter (Excuse me, Graham): The lax and loosening—still discipline in our schools. What follows here, then, is the sad and disastrous tale of what has happened to our two older children as they matriculated at the local high school, one covering grades 7 to 12. (A poor idea, that, combining

7th and 8th graders, students usually beset by all manner of biologic awkwardness, with the much more mature seniors.) It is the story of a boxing match with no end. It is the story of two parents' grief and rising anger at the wretched treatment accorded to their children. Every day, even still, we worry what new cruel conflict or mean word will befall our children. It is, too, the story of school officials who either do not recognize the severity of the problem, or who lack the proper and necessary tools, here St. Joseph's missing hammer, to fix it. And, finally, it is the very discouraging, if not pitiful, inadequacy of the state's educational bureaucracy to solve the problem. Constantly, as you will soon read, our trustful and cogent complaints and entreaties on behalf of our children were routinely met with evasions, obstructions, obfuscations, and, most often, good old-fashioned silence. Perhaps, like many a past ruler, they, those in charge of our children's education, thought that we would go away or, less plausibly, that the condition, like a teenager's bad case of acne, would one day disappear. Silence is a beleaguered bureaucrat's most commonly used weapon; however, as you may surmise, it did not work so well against us. Here is the key: The race for what is just goes not to the quickest or most clever but to whomever has the greater steely determination and endurance. And, all the time, "it is as well to try": <u>Bene</u> <u>est</u> <u>tentare</u>, as is said in Latin.

So, then, I have dallied too long and have thrown too many stones. The Italians might say: Let us leave this: <u>Il</u> <u>sassaila</u> <u>irlandese</u>, the Irish hail of stones. Enough sassaila: enough stones: It is time to tell the tale, a sad one which bears well the talking but which, like any other crop, must be reaped. So . . .

Not long after our daughter entered Toad Lagoon High School as a sophomore, she was involved in a fist fight in the classroom around 8:30 am. I do not know who threw the first punch, perhaps it was one of those fights that simultaneously combusted. Also, since I was not there, I do not know who said what, or when. Yet, soon, fists flew! I will not mention the name of the other "young lady" since that would serve no useful purpose. I did tell the school officials that the other girl had obvious trouble controlling her temper and ought to have, immediately, extensive counseling to combat that problem. As usual, ut solet, I was ignored. It is not good to be constantly ignored or treated as an imbecile or as someone completely unqualified to speak.

The other young lady comes from a broken home, and I think, if I may speculate, that this fact informs some of her anger. She looks around at the other kids from stable and happier homes and is understandably envious. Thus, she asks: Why can't I have parents who are still married to each other and who treat each other decently? If a single mom takes a series of live-in boyfriends, why would the child listen to or respect this new source of discipline? Perhaps he will not even try to be a stern or firm figure, since he, too, came from a broken home. Thus, the disintegration of the family that we have witnessed from the 60's has lead to a deterioration of authority in the home which, in turn, now leads to a lack of respect in the school.

It used to be back in the days when, if you had a transistor radio, you were a techno-geek, that if you got in trouble at school, when you went home, it only got worse, much worse. That is, first Sister Saint Anne would yell at me, and then my dad. I call this the famous double-cheeseburger effect. Now, all is changed: When school officials call home to tell of a child's misbehavior, the parents argue, defending their child, alleging that he has done nothing, though, obviously they will conclusively know nothing of the situation since they were not there. By the way, school officials commonly use this triangular dynamic to defend their lack of efforts in stopping bullying and hazing.

To return to the school, a while later, the other young lady went to a football game and used profane language. She was banned from all future games. I do not know if she has gone through needed counseling or seen a priest. I have heard, though cannot confirm, that she is no longer in school. She is no doubt free to roam, or, as Satre writes, "She is condemned to be free." Apparently, few rules or guidelines or commandments or strictures or customs or morals or mores guide her life. Rather, desire reigns. Thus, she is buffeted about, like a caravel on a very windy day, carrying too much sail. She ought to luff closer to the shore, to feel less strongly all the various winds of desire: Ponente, la bora, greco, austro, libeccio, tramontana, and all the diverse others. So many varying and powerful desire push her around the sea. How can she ever control them, or do they control her?

I wish her no harm. I wonder how to help her, or what to say. Would she listen to me, to anyone? I hope she does nothing stupid, and does not hurt herself or anyone else. My father used to say that there is nothing sadder than seeing a teenager go down the wrong path. He was right.

Now, turning slightly away to another part of the debate, many teachers (not all, not all) will use the breakdown of the family to excuse themselves, to refrain from exacting proper discipline. Some moan: Parents do not demand correct behavior at home, so why are we expected to do all of it in the schools? And, of course, they are, these shirkers, largely right; but, they made a useless point. Yes, support is lacking in the homes; however, the job: To guide youth, to instill a respect for authority, must still be done, ever if more difficult! And yes, it is harder now, with communities full of single moms and divorce and temporary, live-in-boyfriends; yet, the task must still, nevertheless, be accomplished.

Next, of course, we see parents (like me, like me) blaming the lax and ever looser schools for not doing their job. Thus, clearly, unprofitably, each side blames the other. It is the classic, Mexican stand-off. (Excuse me, all those with hyper-sensitive antenna for the politically correct; the fieldworker Mexicans with whom I worked in the orange groves of California actually liked that term: "Mexican stand-off" because it meant that they were tough). It is also what my father used to call, ever since I was 4 years old, the "triangle" or that quick and clever gambit to "always blame the guy not in the room". In other words, that nearly ubiquitous tendency to not take responsibility for one's actions but, rather, to attempt to shift the blame to someone else.

Let us return to the best part, the fight. (I jest, before anyone mocks, I jest, since, if one cannot find a small measure of pleasing mirth within this tale, it does fast grow ever darker). Our daughter was shaken, badly, and complained of right shoulder pain. As I drove her to the hospital not far away to be looked at by a doctor, to make sure that nothing was broken, I asked her, as any proud and protective father might, "Did you land any good ones?" She quickly smiled and said, "Absolutely"! "Good,"

I said, "good". It turns out, happily, that our daughter's physical injuries were relatively minor; though it was the emotional or psychic harm that would linger.

At this point, my wife and I screwed up: we did not raise enough fractious hell! We should have made an instant war-cry, or <u>clamor</u> <u>bellicus</u>. We should have gone straight to the superintendent and demanded to know how, under his watch, this awful soft of thing could have happened. Why did someone not stop the fight as soon as it started? We should have been very stern and very alarmed. We should pointedly have asked him if he were asleep at the helm?

Instead, we assumed, falsely, that the incident was a one-off, an aberration, something quirky which would never happen again. Soon, stupidly, we more or less forgot about the fight, and we and our daughter settled in for the remainder of the school year.

Meanwhile, our daughter had been given a cellphone. I protested this gift since I allowed to my wife that they were only sued by teenagers to purchase drugs, to gossip, to tease and to make dates with boys who, as we all know, are not to be trusted. Most teenage boys, it is clear, and even in this gay-tolerant if not gay-encouraging world, think and ponder and muse and internally dream (those dreams taking the form of nocturnal emissions if all goes according to Hoyle), of only one thing: To achieve entrance to the pleasuring portals of the female body. Despite the fact that with a daughter, I have had to worry about <u>all</u> the dicks in town, I was overruled. Please excuse the old joke but that is the way this old mind leans. As Shakespeare writes, "Mirthful comic shows". (<u>King</u> <u>Henry</u> <u>IV</u>, <u>Part</u> <u>III</u>; V, 7, 43).

Nearly everyone assumed, when cellphone appeared on the scene quickly becoming <u>de regueur</u>, especially for teenage girls, that they were entirely safe, that they would never be used to taunt or harass. Alas! Apples! The cart is upset! That Spring of '08 our daughter started to receive many nasty voice mails and the crudest text message. Certain girls within an amorphous and ever-expanding clique thought it their social duty to do so. Time passed. And that June the ineffectual superintendent resigned citing health reasons, claiming too much pressure.

Cellphones are not supposed to be used during the school day, but of course, that prohibition is roundly and insistently ignored. Students routinely text other during class, and sometimes the messages are harassing or pornographic, sometimes merely distracting. Why did we ever assume it would be any different? Foolishness! In any case cellphones are counter to education; they are anathemas to learning. Yet, today, not just at Toad Lagoon High School but near everywhere, they are common. Their distracting and deleterious effect on knowledge's acquisition cannot be over stressed.

So, what condition marks this debate? Apathy. Apathy is everywhere! We, as parents and administrations, have given immature teenagers the right to carry and use a cellphone and, when they misuse them, we do nothing. This appalling condition that we allow is harming education across our country every day, but who among us raises any loud voice of protest?

Soon after our daughter returned to school that Fall of 2008, her right front car tire was slashed. Not seeing the puncture, and at that point not very familiar with automobiles generally, she started to make the 12-mile drive home. Because of the nearly zero pressure in the tire, the car handled poorly: She could easily have drifted or swerved into the oncoming lane of traffic and been killed! Eventually, she pulled over to the side of the road and stopped. Using her cellphone (properly!), she called for help and received the same. Finally, she came home, shaken and disturbed: Who would do such a thing? Aren't schools suppose to be safe bastions of learning, apart from the ugly fray? Was there a connection to the earlier, and continuing, nasty phone messages: "You are a slut", "Your mom is a whore", etc.? We began to get very upset. We began to realize that the problem of bullying and hazing was much larger and more pervasive than anyone knew and that ignoring the issue was a clear symptom of a deeper crisis.

Armed with the slashed tire, angry and steamed, I went to see Mrs. Ostrich. A long time school employee, the first thing she talked about was how hard her job was. To stop bullying and hazing is practically impossible, she alleged. This was not the sort of comment I wished to hear. "Why don't you have teachers, preferably larger men, stationed outside at the close of the day?" I asked. Why don't you have policemen patrol the halls during the day to prevent mischief, i.e., drug sales, heckling, pushing, and shoving?" I queried. To all of my pressing questions she had the same lame rebuttal. "We can't." or "That is not possible." or "The D.A. must first get involved" and the like were her essentially passive answers. I thought back to my Physics class at Villanova under Fr. Jack Pejza and his phase: "the power of inertia."

That day she reminded me of an ostrich. Let's turn to Brewer's Dictionary of Phrase and Fable:

"At one point the ostrich was fabled, when hunted, to run a certain distance and then thrust its head into the sand, thinking because it cannot see (my emphasis) that it cannot be seen; hence the application of ostrich-like . . . to various forms of self-delusion.
(Cassell; London; 1988; p. 817)

I do not wish to be overly critical of her, but only to stress her essential passivity and also that, wirra, she seemed, and seems, entirely unequipped to fix the vast and spreading problem.

Moreover, let us obvert the issue a dot or whit. To fix permanently any difficult problem requires a 4-stage attack:

1) To diagnose the issue (most difficult).
2) To prescribe and carry out the treatment (carefully).
3) To monitor results after a decent amount of time (taxing).
4) To re-diagnose and re-prescribe as needed (often forgotten).

With regards to bullying and hazing we are still stuck before item #1, a despicable state considering that we are spending Gargantuan sums of monies on public education.

To deter, if one goes back to my high school years in the late 60's, assuredly we are not even in the same financial order of magnitude, and I was lucky enough to study four years of English, four years of Math, two years of Latin, four years of French and History, and four years of the "hard" Sciences. Additionally, though not very talented athletically, I was offered the chance to play all sorts of sports. We had no "soft" classes, no Advanced Placement Classes, no A+'s, no grade inflation, no study halls and very little hazing. What little I saw was immediately squelched. All of this took place at my high school, Villanova Preparatory School run by the rigorous Agustinians who took no guff if you decided, foolishly, to cross them; and, all of this education and rigor and equipment and training and memorization cost a whooping $550 per annum. It is sad and perplexing to compare that school to Toad Lagoons's version of today to which we now return.

Thinking of Mrs. Ostrich, perhaps it is not true that she is an ostrich. Perhaps she recognizes the problem and only wishes it would silently, inexplicably depart; yet, wishing alone will not make it so. All across the country, I would wager, are other principals and teachers similarly befuddled by the problem. They simply do not know where to start. Meanwhile, the ship, she only takes on more water and risks being swamped.

Perhaps the reader has begun to think that I am clearly guilty of the Italian crime of <u>oltraggio</u>, the venal act of insulting a public servant (a reference found in R.J.B. Bosworth's book <u>Mussolini's Italy: Life Under the Fascist Dictatorship</u>, 1915-1945; The Penguin Press; New York; 2006; p. 546), that I protest and excoriate too much, or that all the problems of the school flaw from the breakdown of the family. To that understandable thrust, I must make this return salvo: Too often I have heard Mrs. Ostrich talk first about how difficult the job of defusing bullying and hazing is. That attitude will never work. Never. Since I am my determined father's son, I know that a person must do two things when confronted by <u>any</u> difficult or vexing problem:

> 1) Double one's efforts. Do not give in! Develop perseverance and endurance to the point of a visceral fierceness. Never quit!
> 2) As the difficulty of a problem elevates (think of a Gordian knot, one that must be sliced through), <u>at the same time and until it is vanquished</u>, one must use ever more clean-cut language to solve the problem. Waffling, obscurities, fingers-pointing, and endless, unfocused, fuddled studies only make it worse. And, that is where, unfortunately, we stand today.

So, then, exacerbated by Mrs. Ostrich's listlessness, her wan disinclination towards any strenuous effort, I turned to the new Superintendent, a Mr. Penguin. Surely, he being a feisty Scot (or so I surmised!), he would attach the problem head-on, vigorously, intractably, and without reserve.

However, when I met with him at his fairly plush office, the main message to me was (and here I paraphrase): "This is a difficult problem. My hands are tied. I wish I could do more. We are refocusing our efforts, but some bullying and hazing is going to take place since we are dealing with teenagers." Hardly a call to battle, I thought, or a bright example of resolve. The only time he seemed at all focused was when I told him that our daughter would defend herself with our blessing if she were again attacked. He said, "Oh, no. You can't do that!" There, I crossed him and said that our daughter would not throw the first punch but that she would throw the second. He was not pleased since I had so blatantly contested his authority. I told him that we would not have our girl be a punching bag and on that note our meeting ended.

That meeting was approximately two years ago, and since then, I have only spoken to him on this issue once: We had a very short yelling match! He has never called our house to gauge our feelings, or to give to us the latest update or to register a protest or warning. So much for communication! So much for a superintendent grappling with a tough issue!

Some time passed. Our daughter, still shaken by the tire slashing incident, began to receive an even greater deluge of nasty voice mails and text messages from some anonymous former girlfriend. She had, thankfully, dropped out of that clique because she strongly objected to their habit of smoking. Apparently, they took umbrage at this "small offense", and the rate of salacious messages increased alarming. Our daughter began to see one of the school's counselors, and, at one of their meetings, after our daughter said that she did not feel either safe or comfortable at the school, the counselor suggested that perhaps our daughter ought to drop out for a time, since it was true that her safety could not be guaranteed.

Here we have a situation wherein, even after spending $20,000 per student per year surrounded by scores of teachers, aids, counselors, coaches, deans of discipline, our daughter was not safe. Not surprisingly, her grades began to dip a little since she was so preoccupied by these vicious words and events, and not long afterward she was no longer enrolled at Toad Lagoon High School. She has spent her time recently completing the required courses online and via fax. So much for the thought that she was to spend three years at the school, studying well in a stress free, caring environment, learning much, and making close friends with whom she would be in contact till her waning days. What a failure, we thought.

Annoyed by Penguin's apparent inaction and inability to grappler vigorously with the problem, we decided to go public. Neither our daughter nor we, her parents, have received one word of apology, either in writing or verbally, from anyone involved. We thought: Perhaps a letter writing campaign would put enough pressure on him and Mrs. Ostrich so that they would finally get going, rethink the issue, go outside of the box for a change. I began to write the local police chief and newspapers, the Director of Education (first a Doctor Mills, then a Doctor Steiner), the local district attorney (to alert him to possible threats of violence), in short, anyone whom I thought might help solve the problem. Since I could not, to make a football analogy, run off-tackle, I would make an end around!

What follows then is a chronological selection of much of that bitter correspondence. Most of it is self-explanatory, or so I hope. I have eliminated all names of the teenagers involved, since they are youths, yet I have let the adults' names remain in print since, I figured, they can take it. I have altered a few of the letters slightly, to clarify meaning or avoid repetition; please excuse their often strident tone, and know that it is impossible to avoid if one's child is involved.

Towards the conclusion of these letters, I will warn you now, our young and lanky son enters the fray. (I, too, used to be skinny, but now the panza grows, it only grows.) Entering 7th grade, almost immediately, he was subjected to other types of bullying and hazing: He wasn't sent nasty emails and his car tire wasn't slashed (he is too young to drive!); instead, he was pushed and shoved and told that he likes to sleep with men. Some miscreant said to him, "I want to bang your sister!" One must ask oneself: What has happened to our once civil society? As my wife and I began to wade more deeply into this issue of bullying and hazing we quickly understood that it is much more serious and ubiquitous than either of us, or society as a whole, knows. And, unless we fix it, thoroughly and altogether, our schools and, therefore, our country is lost. And by fixing it, I mean elimination since nothing less will do!

Chapter Two: Rough and Ready

Rough and Ready: Rough in manner but prompt in action; not elaborated, roughly adequate. General Zachary Taylor (1784-1860), twelfth present of the United States, was called Old Rough and Ready, a name he won in the Seminole wars.

Brewer's p. 969

Clearly this phrase was chosen because this contest between the Martins and the school, between passivity and action, between the old guard and the new guard, is a battle just like any other, mean and unruly, and like any other battle it requires tenacity, endurance, and wit.

Letter to the Editor
11/24/2008
Mr. Dan McClelland, Editor
Toad Lagoon Free Press
136 Park Street
Toad Lagoon, NY 12986

Dear Mr. Dan McClelland, Editor:

The residents of Toad Lagoon ought to know that bullying and hazing at the high school is more or less out-of-control. Too many administrators only speak about how difficult the problem is to solve; but, I ask, how hard is it to assign a Toad Lagoon Policeman to the hallways? How difficult would it be to move the largest teacher on staff to the 2nd floor where many problems occur? Too many disciplinary problems have been allowed to sprout and take hold, and now many teachers, having given up old-fashioned tactics (a dose of fear, a sprinkling of intimidation), in response to these hate-filled actions, recommend only passivity and counseling. Pitiful! What about tracking down the thugs and culprits and administering a judicious punishment? Deference: Can anyone say the word?

Dominic Martin

From the "Adirondack Daily Enterprise" dated 1/6/209, Saranac Lake, New York

Heading: Parents argues with school over slashed tires at TL School by Nathan Brown

Dominic Martin, father of former high school student Emily Martin, addressed the Toad Lagoon school board Monday evening, criticizing school officials for failing to find the students who allegedly slashed the tires on his daughter Emily's car in the school parking lot last year.

District officials countered that they followed the law, reported the incident to the police and did everything they could.

Martin said his daughter, while admitting she wasn't blameless in the situation, had been the victim of bullying for a while, receiving nasty text messages and even getting into a fistfight last year.

"Why was she singled out?" he asked. "Because she's new to the town? Perhaps because she lives in a big house?"

Emily Martin is no longer a student at Toad Lagoon middle-high school; district officials said her parents sent her to an equestrian training program in Florida.

Martin said he approached the school with a list of suspects and that, in past years, the principal would have brought those students in "for a long and blistering inquisition." Now, though, he said, "the kids run the school, not the administration," and the district needs to bring back "a little fear and intimidation so these creeps will obey. If pushy is what it takes to catch this jerk, that's a good word."

District Superintendent Seth Penguin said the school is a public facility, bound by state laws, and it would not be possible to confront the suspects the way Martin suggested.

"We can't be bullying the bullies," Penguin said.

Penguin said what happened was a criminal act and that district officials talked to the police and turned over all evidence to them.

"There are a number of erroneous statements (Martin) made." Penguin said. "We are stepping up measures all the time to address these sort of issues."

From Toad Lagoon Free Press on 1/7/2009, Toad Lagoon, New York

Heading: Parent of bullied teen presses board for justice; officials say matter fully investigated

A parent who claims his teenage daughter's car had the tires slashed in the school parking lot and she was bullied in school for over a year asked the board of education for justice for his daughter Monday night.

High School Principal Mrs. Ostrich said while the entire incident is very unfortunate, her office "investigated it as thoroughly as it could," including a joint investigation with the village police.

Superintendent of schools Seth Penguin said that everything was done that could be done to help the student.

Dominic Martin, who contended in a letter to the editor in the Free Press on November 26 (sic: 24) that bullying and hazing is "more or less out of control" at the high school, appeared before the board during the open comment portion of Monday's regular meeting.

He told the board that his daughter, while a student at Toad Lagoon High, had the tires on her car slashed while it was parked on school grounds. More important to him, however, was his claim that his daughter had been the victim of bullying and harassment by fellow students for a year and a half. Much of that bullying came in the form of "nasty text messages," he said.

He admitted, however, his daughter wasn't blameless in the exchange of communications during her time at the high school.

His daughter is currently living in Florida pursuing equestrian studies, as well as completing her high school studies here via fax and e-mail.

"We miss our daughter," he told the board, and explained that her inability to attend school here "deprives her of normal high school relationships with her friends."

He wondered why the bullying issue at the high school is so difficult for administrators to address.

Mr. Martin said there is "a conspiracy of silence" present in the school administration "that mocks justice." He said he couldn't believe the culprits responsible have not yet been found and reprimanded.

"Years ago if a principal was given the names of culprits," they would have been brought into the principal's office and disciplined, he told the board members.

"What has happened to authority and discipline in our school? Why haven't the people responsible been caught and punished?"

Mr. Martin claimed that if district administrators used the old tactics of "fear and intimidation" it would go a long way to driving "the creeps" out of school.

Later in the meeting after his departure, School Board Member John Quinn asked the school administrators to explain what has been done about the incident.

Superintendent Penguin said Mr. Martin had made "a number of erroneous statements "in his presentation, including a point that Emily Martin "was asked not to return to school."

"The school would never ask a student not to return!" He said she is taking special equestrian training in Florida, as she has done in the past.

"As an administration we have done everything we were asked to do," Mr. Penguin told the board. On school bullying in particular, "we are stepping up measures all the time" to combat it.

He said he understood a little of Mr. Martin's concern. "As a parent, it's heartbreaking if you think your child is somehow being attacked!"

Board Vice President Pat Facteau was upset by the tire slashing, in particular, which he called a criminal act.

Mr. Penguin said he has had several discussions with the village police—"and the investigation was done as it should have been done."

Board President Mike Dechene said when the board members first received a letter from Mr. Martin, they immediately turned over the matter to school administrators to investigate fully. He said they took Mr. Martin's concerns very seriously.

"We have a zero tolerance policy on bullying. Are we going to prevent all of it, however? Probably not!"

Letter to the Editor

Mr. Dan McClelland, Editor
Toad Lagoon Free Press
136 Park Street
Toad Lagoon, NY 12986

Dear Mr. Dan McClelland, Editor:

On November 4, 2008 our daughter had her car tire slashed while her car was parked on the Toad Lagoon High School grounds. This act stemmed from the hazing and bullying that obviously is prevalent at the school despite the denials of school officials.

Now, nearly seven months have passed and yet the culprit remains at large. We fear that he may be a graduating senior, perhaps about to leave the area, and hence this note.

The town police said it would take nine months to solve this crime; horse feathers! Mrs. Ostrich has left one message on our phone; so much for decisive action.

Superintendent Penguin apparently things that after turning the matter over to the ineffectual police that he may wash his hands from the matter. When one of the counselors who works at the school said to us that perhaps we should remove Emily from the school since she cannot be protected, Mr. Penguin called me a liar.

In removing Emily from the school we did what the counselor had suggested. Yet Penguin's answer is to call me a liar. Clearly, he then crossed the line and owes our family an apology.

Forty years ago, I know how this sort of thing would have been handled at my high school, an all-boys Catholic school: The football coach would have said that all games would be cancelled unless the miscreant confesses. That old fashioned strategy would have worked in days!

The little creep who did this needs to fess up, for the sake of his conscience and if he wants to be called a man. Maybe I should start going door to door, asking pesky questions, but then again, is that not what the officials are meant to do. The word "lazy" comes to mind.

Sincerely,

Dominic Martin

January 12, 2009

Dr. Richard Mills
Commissioner of Education
New York State Education Department
89 Washington Avenue
Albany, NY 12234

Dear Dr. Mills,

Last year our daughter was hazed continuously at the Toad Lagoon High School. Three weeks ago some miscreant slashed her car tire, a crime as yet unsolved which we wish to prosecute. The point is that discipline has broken down at the high school. The current staff is not the right one to fix the problem. Our daughter has been advised not to return to school. How much money are we spending, no, wasting?

Dominic Martin

Various emails received at the "Adirondack Daily Enterprise" January 13, 2009

"The Martin's are 100% correct in their concerns. I can not imagine being a high school student moving into Toad Lagoon. I moved here about 20 years as an adult and I have yet to be accepted in this town. Toad Lagoon is a beautiful town with a lot to offer a family but if I had to do it over gain I would have chosen to live in a more accepting town. You see, if you don't live here as a young child or do not have relatives here, the natives never truly open-up to your presence. In other words—outsiders are generally not welcome. It would be interesting to know just how many young families who have left town left because one spouse or both were not from Toad Lagoon and never felt part of the community. I can name many who worked in town, coached young children, and volunteered on a regular basis but ended up moving due to the fact that the family and high school connections in Toad Lagoon can never be flexible enough to allow new people in. You are better off in Florida!"

Please check the TLHS web side linked to ADE: this is their mission statement. I guess "accountability for their actions: is missing from this statement . . . ."

It is the mission of the school district and this community to set high exceptions for our youth and provide a well rounded education program to enable our graduates to be productive and successful in their personal and professional lives.

"Well maybe the kids in school just don't like your daughter and as far as Obama's speech in school, what's it gonna hurt, after all, Americans did vote him in as president, did we not. The police should have cameras up to catch the perps slashing the tires, plain and simple."

"Small town think—perhaps the perps who did the tire slashing have the right names and therefore will continue to act as such with the school's blessing."

"Penguin said they can't bully the bullies? Why not? Cut them down in their tracks!"

January 14, 2009

Mr. John D. Delehanty
Chief Assistant District Attorney
56 Lake Street
Toad Lagoon, NY 12986

Dear Mr. Delehanty,

As you perhaps know, our 16 year old daughter, Emily Martin, had her car tire slashed while it was parked at the Toad Lagoon High School. The date was November 4, 2008. We filed a police report and they are apparently investigating, but this action is occurring way too slowly: The culprit is still at large two months after the crime!

The point of this note is to ask you to put some pressure on the Toad Lagoon Police Department to act more decisively. The police may tell you that I irretrievably harmed their investigation but that may be because they are looking for an excuse for not doing their job! I went to one of the possible suspects home to investigate, as any alarmed parent might, asking only the <u>most polite</u> questions. Shortly afterwards, one of the police officers called to yell at me and to tell us that this case would take 9 months to solve. Hogwash!

Meanwhile, our daughter was told by officials at the school to not return to the high school since her safety could not be guaranteed. Obviously, bullying and hazing at the high school is a big, and unsolved, problem. The current techniques used to try to get rid of this type of aggression are clearly not working. The only consistent statement that we have heard from both school and police officials is this: This is a difficult problem." That's simply not good enough! Anything that you can do to get to the bottom of this issue would be much appreciated.

Sincerely,
Dominic Martin

Letter from Office of Franklin County District Attorney

January 16, 2009

Dominic Martin
334 State Route 421
Toad Lagoon, New York 12986

Re: Yours of January 14, 2009

Dear Mr. Martin:

Thank you for your referenced correspondence. I have contacted the village of Toad Lagoon Police Department to make them aware of your concerns regarding the investigation of the criminal mischief to your daughter Emily's Motor vehicle on November 4, 2008.

I am sure that as a victim of a crime, you have grave concern over not only the offense perpetrated against your family member's property but also regarding how long it sometimes takes to solve a case. In your letter you told me that you apparently attempted to investigate this matter yourself and went to who you believed to be a possible suspect's home and asked questions.

Our office frowns upon this sort of self-help by victims of offence. The appropriate response to this offense was to, as you did, file a police report. From that point it is the duty of sworn law enforcement officials to proceed with an investigation in order to ascertain whether or not the case may be closed by an arrest. When a case is thus "closed by arrest" it is the District Attorney's obligating to proceed with viable prosecutions.

Involvement by victims in investigating crimes against family members only exposes those victims and their families to potential further harm (retaliation) and jeopardizes professional investigation by law enforcement. It also makes prosecution by our Office much more difficult because the rules of evidence are such that proof beyond a reasonable doubt, being such a high standard, is diminished when a jury may believe that a family vendetta is involved. It also minimizes a juror's natural inclination to have empathy for a victim of an offense.

Should you have any questions or concerns, please give me a call or drop me a line. I also took the liberty of sharing your letter with the Guidance Office at Toad Lagoon High School, since you portrayed other matters regarding the school district in the letter.

Very truly yours,

John D. Delehanty

To: Darryl L. Daily
   New York State Education
   Department
   Safe Schools and Alternative
   Education Team
   89 Washington Avenue
   Albany, New York 12234

and

To: All Members of the Toad Lagoon
   Board of Education

On November 4, our daughter, then a junior here, had her car tire slashed while it was parked on the high school grounds. We are pursuing an investigation through the Toad Lagoon Police Department. We want restitution for the damages ($150.00) but, much more than that, a much safer high school where this kind of thing could never happen again, to our child or to any other.

Our daughter experienced bulling and hazy for the entire 1½ years she was here. Last year there was a fist fight. All sorts of nasty text messages have been sent back and forth. Finally, after the tire incident she was not asked back. Today she is finishing her schooling by e-mail and fax from Florida where she has a job. We miss our daughter but also, because of the lack of discipline here at the high school, she is being deprived of the normal, varied friendships that a normal high school should allow. By the way, in 2 months Chief Fie has not called, Officer Schiff called to yell at me, and Mrs. Ostrich left one message after we called her.

As we pursued this case, all involved, the police and the school officials spoke first and primarily about how hard their job is. We say: If it is so difficult, quit! Let's get some people here who will vigorously pursue the culprit, instead of complaining and whining about how hard their job is.

Was our daughter singled out because she was new to town or lived in a big house? Those things ought to make no difference! Unfortunately there is a conspiracy of silence here which mocks justice and it must be stopped. The "good ol' boy" network has not caught the culprit and it has been more than two months.

Years ago, if something like this occurred and the principal was given the names of possible suspects, he would have immediately brought each in for a long and blistering inquisition. Now the investigation, such as it is, is carried out by the police department and the kids, noting this triangle, play one side off against the other, running circles around the so-called experts.

This sort of thing can't stand! Discipline is for too lax! Whatever happened to authority and discipline judiciously applied? Why can't the police or the teachers stop the lying which covers up the crime? Answer: The kids run the school, not the administration. Why has the kid who did this not been found and punished? Why has he not learned the lesson of accountability: That if he does something wrong, he will be caught and punished. Behind that grin, he smirks.

It is time to "Bring Back." Bring back a little fear. Bring back some intimidation so that these creeps will be compelled to obey. As the late Tim Russert writes, "We are so eager to be understanding and sympathetic that we end up being too lenient, even as we further undermine the already diminished authority of teachers, coaches and principals."[1]

And please don't say how had the job is. Some people are just cashing the paycheck and are not vigorous investigators and yes, pushy enough. If "pushy" is what it takes to catch this jerk, good! Our daughter could have been killed.

---

[1]   From Big Russ and Me. Tim Russert; Hyperion, New York; 2004; p. 190.

Letter from The State Education
Department / The University of the State
of New York

January 23, 2009

Dominic & Catherine Martin
334 State Route 421
Toad Lagoon, New York 12986

Dear Mr. Martin,

Thank you for providing an update regarding your presentation to the board of education concerning your daughter being a victim of hazing and bullying and the continuing safety issue at Toad Lagoon High School.

As mentioned in my previous correspondence on December 8 2008, I made suggestions for you to follow. It seems that you had followed the guidance provided in that document.

I wish you all the best with your continued efforts. If you have any further questions or concerns you could contact me at (518) 486-6090 or DDAILY@MAIL.NYSED.GOV.

Respectfully,

Darryl L. Daily

February 2009

From the Desk of Principal Mrs. Ostrich . . .

We are half-way through the 2008-2009 school year, and with the new year come new challenges. Our new President recently said, "our challenges may be new. The instruments with which we meet them may be new. But those values upon which our success depends—hard work and honestly, courage and fair play, tolerance and curiosity, loyalty and patriotism—these are things of old. These things are true. They have been the quiet force of progress throughout our history. What is demanded then is to return to these truths. What is required of us now is a new era of responsibility—a recognition on the part of every American, that we have duties to ourselves, our nation and the world, duties that we do not grudgingly accept but rather seize gladly, firm in the knowledge that there is nothing so satisfying to the spirit, so defining of our character, than giving our all to a difficult task."

I believe that a safe, positive, and caring environment fosters learning and as Principal, I work hard to ensure that the Middle High School has this type of environment. Harassment and bullying are problems at many public school, particularly at the secondary level. We try to address every reported incident of bullying and harassment in a timely manner, while teaching that you will also assist us by reminding your sons and daughters to be kind, honest, hard working and tolerant of each other.

January 19, 2009

Mr. John D. Delehanty
Chief Assistant District Attorney
56 Lake Street
Toad Lagoon, NY 12986

Dear Mr. Delehanty,

Thank you for your note of January 16, 2009.

I would like to point out that you spent most of your time criticizing me, rather than addressing the real crime that was committed. Surely, what I did was what any alarmed and persistent father, faced with a fundamental passivity of all officials involved, would have done. Also, what I did would have been expected behavior, say, when we were children forty years ago because back then the scale of justice had not veered towards the culprit, as they have today.

There lurks at the high school some lying, smirking student who has gotten away with this crime. The only real question is this: What are you prepared to do to catch him? It almost seems as if you and all the other officials involved, side with the criminal and not the victim who happened to be our daughter. Having just learned how to drive a car, our daughter could have been killed. Does anyone care about that?

You must know that more than a year ago, or daughter was involved in a fist fight at the high school. Despite the protests of the police department, who did not think it important, we filed a police report.

It is time for the teachers and administrators to bring back some of the disciplinary tools necessary to reinstate order in the school. Otherwise, the foxes will continue to guard the chicken coop.

Sincerely,

Dominic Martin

P.S. I am sending a copy of all letters relating to this issue to District Attorney Derek Champagne in Malone in the perhaps futile hope that he can get something done. Nine months to solve? Can't bully the bullies? How would you like it to be your daughter? If we cannot get this crime solved, we will contact the State Attorney General Andrew Cuomo.

February 22, 2009

District Attorney Derek P. Champagne
355 West Main Street
Malone, NY 12953

Dear District Attorney Champagne,

Before I forget, I wanted to send to you the copy of the bill relating to the repair of Emily Martin's slashed tire.

We hope this case gets solved and thank you for your efforts.

Sincerely,

Dominic

Email to: Dominic Martin

From: Darryl L. Daily
New York State Education Department

Dated: June 4, 2009

Dear Mr. Martin,

This email serves as a follow up to our conversation yesterday concerning your situation with your daughter and the Toad Lagoon High School. You mentioned that although your daughter is taking courses now in NYC as a result of being bullied in the school you were concerned with the way the school administration and local police continues to handle hazing and bullying issues. I shared with you the most recent formal complaint process. As requested I am sending you a complaint form that is attached. As discussed, I asked that you fill out the form in it's (sic) entirety. Please sign the portion of the form that gives us permission to reveal your name to the district as you stated you are fine with. Once you send the form to us then I would contact the school and they would have ten days to respond to your compliant. If you have any questions or concerns you can reach me at the numbers provided below:

Respectfully,

Darryl L. Daily
New York State Education Department
Safe Schools and Alternative Education
Team
89 Washington Avenue
Room 318 M-EB
Albany, New York 12234

Office: (518)486-3640
Direct Line: (518)473-1233
Cell: (518)330-5722
DDAILY@mail.NYSED.GOV
Fax (518)474-8299
http://www.emsc.nysed.gov/ssae/

June 5, 2009

Darryl L. Daily
New York State Education Department
Safe Schools and Alternative Education
Team
89 Washington Avenue
Albany, New York 12234

Dear Mr. Daily,

As requested, here is the form filled
out. Hard copy to follow. Thanks for your
efforts. This lack of discipline in the high
school here has been going on for far too
long.

Sincerely,

Dominic Martin

Official Complaint Filed with New York State Education Department:

June 5, 2009

1. Describe the concerns that led you to file this complaint. Be sure to include all important information including the date of the alleged incident.

On November 4, 2008 our daughter had her car tire slashed while it was parked in the high school grounds. This stemmed from many bullying and hazing incidents going back to the previous school year. We immediately complained to both Mrs. Ostrich & Penguin, and the first thing that they both said was how difficult it is to solve the problem. Penguin called me a liar since we elected to take our daughter out of the school (a counselor's recommendation) and Mrs. Ostrich left only one message.

2. State your proposed resolution of the problem. State what you would suggest NYSED do to resolve this issue.

My wife, Kate, and I both believe that Mrs. Ostrich should go. She is a perfect example of the Peter Principle, and here's why: students routinely text each other in school. The school dress code is unenforced. Students flaunt the "No Smoking" rule by smoking just off campus. When teachers do discipline a student, often Mrs. Ostrich undercuts them, and especially the female teachers. Our daughter alleges that drugs are often sold out of the second floor lockers. The graudation rate for the school is low and many good students, their parents fearful for their welfare, have transferred out. As Gen. Bradley said to Gen. Patton after the debacle of Kasserine Pass, "Discipline is pretty poor." "She should go."

Letter From Darryl L. Daily
The State Education Department/
University of the State of New York
Albany, NY 12234

June 4, 2009

Mr. and Mrs. Dominic Martin
344 State Route 421
Toad Lagoon, New York 12986

Dear Mr. Martin,

Thank you for your continuous updates concerning the manner in which the Toad Lagoon High School handled your daughter's hazing and bullying case. You expressed to me that although your daughter is now finishing school through correspondence courses from NYC, you are concerned with the way the district handled her case. In addition, you expressed concern with the safety and welfare of current and future students within the district as a result of your experiences.

In our previous correspondence I suggested that you follow the chain of command and keep detailed documentation of your communication with the school district. You did follow this guidance as demonstrated in the letters you provided. When I contacted you by telephone yesterday, I shared with you a most recent formal complaint process that you can fill out and send back to me.

I encourage you to fill out the complaint in its entirety. As discussed, please sign where it allows or denies permission to reveal your name to the district. After receiving the form I will then contact the school about your complaint. The school will then have 10 days to respond to the complaint.

Thank you for your concern with the safety of our children in New York State. If you have any further questions or concerns, you can contact me at (518) 473-1233 or DDAILY@MAIL.NYSED.GOV.

Respectfully,

Darryl Daily
cc: J.C. Stevens
        G. Bayduss

Supporting Deposition
Toad Lagoon Police Department
June 5, 2009

I, Dominic M. Martin, am 57 years of age, my date of birth is 10/xx/xxxx, and I reside at 334 State Rt 421 Toad Lagoon New York 12986. The date is 6/5/09 and the time is 3:00 pm and I now make the following statement. That I am at the Toad Lagoon Police Department speaking to officer Griffin about the incident that took place on November 13, 2008 at the Toad Lagoon High School parking lot. That my daughter was driving a 2000 BMW station wagon to school that day and while the vehicle was parked the front passenger side tire was slashed damaging the tire. At no time was there ever permission given to anyone to do damage [to] said tire. I would like any and all person involved with this crime arrested for what they did.

Letter to the Editor at the Adirondack Daily Enterprise dated Friday, May 29, 2009

Heading: Police, school officials don't seem to care

To the editor:

On Nov. 4, 2008, our daughter, Emily Martin, had her care tire slashed while her car was parked on the Toad Lagoon Middle-High School grounds. This act stemmed from the hazing and bullying that, obviously, is prevalent at the school, despite the denials of school officials. Now, nearly seven months have passed, and yet the culprit, a punk, remains at large. We fear that he may be a graduating senior, perhaps about to leave the area, and hence, this note.

The village police said it would take nine months to solve this crime. Horse feathers! Mrs. Ostrich (no relation) has left one message on our phone; so much for decisive action. Superintendent Penguin apparently thinks that, after turning the matter over to the ineffectual police, that he may wash his hands of the matter. When one of the counselors who works at the school said to us that perhaps we ought to remove our daughter from the school, since she cannot be protected, Penguin called me a liar. Clearly, he then crossed a line and owes our family an apology.

Forty years ago, I know how this sort of thing would have been handled at my tough, all-boy Catholic school: The football coach would have said that all games would be cancelled unless the miscreant confesses. That old-fashioned strategy would have worked in days!

The little creep who did this needs to fess up, for the sake of his conscience and if he wants to be called a man. Maybe I should start going door to door, asking pesky questions, but, then again, is that not what the officials are meant to do? The word "lazy" comes to mind.

Sincerely,
Dominic Martin
Toad Lagoon

June 9, 2009

Darryl L. Daily
New York State Education Department
Safe Schools and Alternative Education
Team
89 Washington Avenue
Albany, New York 12234

Dear Mr. Daily,

I thought that you ought to know that our daughter entering Toad Lagoon High School as a sophomore in the Fall of 2007 was there for only a couple of months before she was slugged in the classroom around 8 A.M. Because she was brand-new to the school, this hazing and bullying began nearly right away! The police department had to be talked into writing up a report.

Also, last Thursday night the soon-to-be-graduating seniors organized a large party at which alcohol was served. How the school's staff, principal, and superintendent might not have known about this party beforehand is hard to fathom! Perhaps a teacher or two knew and said, "Why bother?" Towards the end of the party, one of the revelers was hit by a car and had to be taken to the hospital. How did they get the alcohol? Why did the police apparently do nothing? Given

the public campaign that teenagers not
drink, this apathy sends all high school
students a very mixed message.

Yours,

Dominic Martin

June 9, 2009

District Attorney Derek P. Champagne
355 West Main Street
Malone, NY 12953

Dear District Attorney Champagne,

I thought you ought to know that back in the Fall of 2007, after just entering Toad Lagoon High school for the first time as a sophomore, our daughter was slugged in the classroom. At first, the local police, disinterested and apathetic, were disinclined to even make a report, but I talked them into it. Emily should have had three good years in school but, because of this ongoing bullying problem, she has had to complete her courses online and by fax, and it that process she has been deprived of many friendships that a normal high school experience would allow.

This last Thursday night a large senior party was held at which alcohol was consumed. Why have a public campaign that teenagers should not drink when this sort of party can take place? Someone was hit by a car and had to be taken to the hospital. Why did the local police apparently look the other way when the law was being broken?

The other day when I filed my report (why the 6 month delay?) the police blamed their lack of success on me—that by my going to ____ house (as any father might!) I permanently botched the investigation. One of the school bus drivers, is now telling Officer Fee that he heard boys on the bus say that _____ slashed my daughter's tire. With this kind of evidence, why has he not been arrested? Is it because we are relatively new to town and not part of the good-old-boy network? Is it because _____'s grandfather was a policeman and that, therefore, he is specially protected? My wife and I are fearful that since _____ is a senior he may be moving away.

I think the police are more mad at me than interested in solving the case. Clearly there is a 2-tier justice system around here and we are on the bottom level. Dear sir, please help.

Yours,

Dominic Martin

June 9, 2009

Darryl L. Daily
New York State Education Department
Safe Schools and Alternative Education
Team
89 Washington Avenue
Albany, New York 12234

Dear Mr. Daily,

More news: Today, our daughter, reports that over the past two night she received four nasty phone calls from:

1) _____ (who slugged her 1 ½ years ago), and

2) _____

Our daughter is crying. Our file on this issue is as thick as a NYC phone book. We insist that she never again enter the high school and that different arrangements be made for her to take the Regent's Exam. Mrs. Ostrich should be fired! Now!

Dominic Martin

June 11, 2009

Superintendent Seth Penguin:
Toad Lagoon High School
294 Hosley Avenue
Toad Lagoon, NY 12986

Dear Superintendent Seth Penguin,

By asking me if Emily did not also possess a cell phone, you implied that she was responsible, partially, for the many attacks against her. Here is the key difference: Emily does not use her cell phone for deleterious effect. Just so you know– I am trying to get Mrs. Ostrich fired—for the good of the town and school. If you don't start applying some serious pressure on the police and knowledgeable students, you are next in line. Emily has been harassed for two years.

Dominic Martin

June 13, 2009

Darryl L. Daily
New York State Education Department
Safe Schools and Alternative Education
Team
89 Washington Avenue
Albany, New York 12234

Dear Mr. Daily,

I apologize for naming two young ladies when that claim cannot be proven. This hazing and bullying has gone on for nearly two years and our daughter's normal high school experience destroyed. We ask for help—from the school administrators, the town police, you—and are mostly ignored; I call it "a conspiracy of silence" or a large circle of finger-pointing. The plain fort is this: A lack of discipline exists at the high school, exacerbated by cell phones usage. Therefore, they should be banned. You must be 18 to own one. Maybe I should write a screenplay or book on this issue. I bet it would sell!

Dominic Martin

June 13, 2009

Superintendent Seth Penguin:
Toad Lagoon High School
294 Hosley Avenue
Toad Lagoon, NY 12986

Dear Superintendent Penguin,

I apologize for naming two names when that claim cannot be proven. I do not apologize for yelling at you, since you need it. You do not yet know how to lead or be a boss. If you did not know about the illegal senior party, or, if you did know, and then did nothing, either way, you should be embarrassed. A lack of discipline exists at the high school, made worse by cellphones, and therefore, they should be banned, that is, if you wish discipline to return. I think you are yellow, afraid to stick your neck out. Pitiful leadership!

Dominic Martin

June 14, 2009

Superintendent Seth Penguin:
Toad Lagoon High School
294 Hosley Avenue
Toad Lagoon, NY 12986

Dear Superintendent Penguin,

Many of your students will graduate having never been exposed to any kind of stern discipline. And, therefore, what will they do when, later, they encounter a tough boss, or a job that is not to their liking? They will shirk the responsibility. Thus, you are not preparing them for the real world, but, rather, raising a good-sized crop of emotional pansies. And, also, in the process, since discipline is so small a part of your job, you are left with considerable less to do: I call it "Getting paid too much for doing so little."

Dominic Martin

June 17, 2009

Superintendent Seth Penguin:
Toad Lagoon High School
294 Hosley Avenue
Toad Lagoon, NY 12986

Dear Superintendent Penguin,

Our daughter, entering Toad Lagoon High School as a sophomore in the Fall of 2007, was not on campus 60 days before she was singled out by some nasty pieces of work and slugged, at 8am, right in a classroom! We filed a police report after I had to talk the police into doing so. Since that time and, now, under your ostrich watch, she has been bullied two more times. In less than two years we have had to go to the police three times! Don't feign surprise at our anger! Many teachers around you are disgusted at your inability or unwillingness to grapple with this problem. Ban cell phones!
Dominic Martin

June 24, 2009

Darryl L. Daily
New York State Education Department
Safe Schools and Alternative Education
Team
89 Washington Avenue
Albany, New York 12234

Dear Mr. Daily,

Good morning! We thought that you ought to know about a couple of new developments. The high school student whom we suspected had committed the tire slashing finally confessed to the town police last week. Secondly, my wife's position at the grammar school (part-time Physical Education teacher, including adaptive PE), save one minor sport, is the only one eliminated among roughly 45-50 teachers and staff at the grammar school. Naturally, we strongly suspect that there is a strong correlation between our outspokenness against bullying and hazing and her being effectively fired. We are not litigious people, but clearly, the possibility of a lawsuit against the school district exists. The point is this: Whatever happened to the First Amendment in our country? We have only tried to help the school, and to get rid of this blight—bullying and hazing—which has so drastically affected our daughter, and, yet, this is the thanks we get? Penguin and Mrs. Ostrich continue to act as if all is well, acting like Mr. Ostrich and Mrs. Ostrich.

Finally, our daughter, two weeks ago received some nasty text messages again! from a girl we suspect is _____ who is the same girl who punched our daughter 1 ½ years ago. This same girl is, apparently, also texting nasty message to another female student. Obviously, _____ needs help: She is very angry and probably needs to be in a special program of some kind. She does not need to be in Toad Lagoon High School free to nasty text message whomever she pleases. She needs help, now, and Penguin and Mrs. Ostrich are not providing it.

Best regards,

Dominic Martin

Letter From Darryl L. Daily

The State Education Department/
University of the State of New York
Albany, NY 12234

June 29, 2009

Mr. and Mrs. Dominic Martin
344 State Route 421
Toad Lagoon, New York 12986

Re: Response

Dear Mr. Martin

The New York State Education
Department has received a response
from Mr. Seth Penguin, Superintendent
of Toad Lagoon Central School District,
and it appears that the school district
used its standard procedures to address
the issues raised in the complaint.
Thus, at this time, the Department does
not require any additional information
from the school district regarding this
matter. However, please be advised that
the Department reserves the right to
reopen this complain if it determines
that it is appropriate to do so.
In moving forward, the Department
continuously encourages parents and
school districts to meet and work

together to resolve any concerns at the local level. Good luck to you and your daughter, and give me a call or e-mail if you need any further assistance. Thank you for contacting the New York State Education Department.

Respectfully,

Darryl L. Daily
Safe Schools and Alternative Education Team
cc: G. Bayduss

July 6, 2009

Dr. Richard Mills
Commissioner of Education
New York State Education Department
89 Washington Avenue
Albany, NY 12234

Dear Dr. Mills,

Last week we received this enclosed note from Mr. Darryl Daily dated June 29 relating to the series of bullying and hazing that our daughter, Emily Martin, has been subjected to over the past two years at Toad Lagoon High School. His responses is pitifully weak and makes me wonder if the Safe School Team is not just a "rubber stamp" for all administrators so that the can keep their jobs no matter how poorly they are performing them.

Nearly two years ago _____ slugged our daughter in the classroom and, just a few weeks ago, we believe, she texted her with nasty and mean messages. The school has demonstrated that it cannot stop her. Clearly, she should be in a special school to control her anger. I am doing you a favor here.

Why are these children allowed to have cellphones in school? Is it not meant to be a place of learning? Why does the principal, Mrs. Ostrich, not confiscate them at the start of the school day? Is it because she acts like an ostrich, putting her head in the sand? Why did she not know beforehand of the illegal senior class party at which much hard liquor was consumed and after which one student was hit by a car? Why does she allow smoking right outside the school? Why are drugs dealt out of the 2nd—floor—lockers? There can only be one answer to all these questions: Mrs. Ostrich is afraid to discipline her students, abdicating that job to some male teachers.

Our special daughter has had a terrible time there, yet she has scarcely received an apology from anyone. As I mentioned, the attached note is pitiful. Also, once again, by continuing to press this issue, we are doing you and your office a favor. Maybe I should write a book about the state's inaction.

Sincerely,

Dominic Martin

Email to Mr. Darryl Daily

June 29, 2009

Dear Mr. Daily,

Thank you for the response to our complaint about the Toad Lagoon High School. We are very unhappy with your response. It is exactly the response that we expected with Mr. Penguin stating that he had used standard procedures. Well, we can tell you—there is nothing standard about this school district. The Superintendent runs the District exactly the way he wants it with no respect for the parents or the police. The police and the district do not communicate well and the district turns all responsibility over to the police with no internal investigation by the school. In the old days, the school sports teams would have been made to cancel all their games until the perpetrator fessed up. But today all the tools have been taken away. We solved the crime of our daughter's tire being slashed by using pressure through the media –i.e. letters to the local paper. The kid eventually caved to the pressure and confessed to his mother. Mr. Penguin then suggested that we do not press charges as he believed the crime not worthy of criminal charges. Thankfully the police disagreed with Mr. Penguin. Mr. Penguin does not like it when someone makes his school look bad in public—he even publicly called me a liar. But it is bad and there is a conspiracy of silence here in Toad Lagoon.

The high school is a joke—the kids run the show and the principal does not discipline—moreover, she sides with the male teachers and makes the lives of most of the female teachers a misery. Teachers who refer kids for dress code infractions or some other problem are ridiculed and made to look ineffective when the unruly student returns to class having not been disciplined at all. For example, if a girl has a low top on she is sent to the office and while in transit she pulls the top up high and covers her flesh so that when she arrives in the office there is suddenly no problem. A presence in and out of the classroom on a regular basis by a "competent administrator" (and there isn't one here) would improve discipline. Teenagers are well-known for getting out of situations since they commonly lie; cellphone usage is rampant as is the selling of drugs out of lockers on the second floor. Bullying and hazing is out of control and no one in the district thinks that it is a problem. Well it is, since or daughter received more harassing text messages three weeks ago, and she is no longer in school. The same girl who beat our daughter up two years ago sent nasty, harassing messages to another girl in the school two weeks ago, but since that girl's mother is an employee trying to gain tenure, nothing was done. We were never told two years ago that we could have pressed charges against that girl and here she is two years later, carrying on with the same behavior. Kids like that need to be expelled—immediately. There is another problem: Employees routinely complain about how awful the superintendent is, and how awful the high school is, but they don't tell people like you about it because they are afraid to lose their job or are made to feel uncomfortable by "Hitler and his wife"—which is what some employees call Mr. Penguin and his wife who is a teacher.

So, of course you are going to side with Mr. Penguin because he says that everything is okay here. But it is not well. Many of the kids just graduated this week tell us that they are so glad to get out of the high school. We have heard that there is a program in New York State which monitors bullying and hazing in schools. You must not be monitoring this high school. Some kids (like our daughter) have left this high school. Some parents are looking at other schools because they do not like what they see.

Maybe it might be a good idea for you to get out of your office and make a surprise is it to Toad Lagoon High School in the Fall and walk the halls and observe the chaos yourself. A response from a superintendent who wears rose colored glasses and has his head in the sand is not good enough. Perhaps you might also consider an anonymous survey amongst the school district employees to see what they have to say about the high school and us—and you and Mr. Penguin might well play a starring role.

Sincerely,

The Martins

July 3, 2009

District Attorney Derek P. Champagne
355 West Main Street
Malone, NY 12953

Dear District Attorney Champagne,

   With respect to _____'s confession of the slashing of our daughter's car tire, now that that admission has been accomplished, we wonder where we stand. We would like restitution and prosecution. Nobody has told us anything since his confession which was 2 or 3 weeks ago. We believe he should be prosecuted since a) this is a serious crime, and b) he lied about it for over 6 months. Please advise at your convenience as to what is to happen.

                Sincerely,

                Dominic Martin

July 3, 2009

Darryl L. Daily
New York State Education Department
Safe Schools and Alternative Education
Team
89 Washington Avenue
Albany, New York 12234

Dear Mr. Daily,

Why were we never told two years ago that we could have pressed charges against _____? Why was the Toad Lagoon Police Department disinclined to take our three reports regarding bullying and hazing? Why, three weeks after _____'s confession, has the DA not told us what is happening with the case? Why did Penguin call me a liar when I was simply doing what his employee, a counselor, suggested? Why does Penguin go out of his way to curry favor with the local press, yet he cannot stop the bullying and hazing? Why does Mrs. Ostrich still have her job even though cell phone usage is rampant? Why does your office do nothing when an illegal senior class party was held at which consumption of hard liquor was common? Why does this "conspiracy of silence" exist? Education in the public sector is no longer about the students' improvement, or standards and discipline; but, rather it is about too many teachers, too much staff, and bloated budgets. Shortly, New York will follow California into bankruptcy. Frankly, you need my help to avoid the advancing calamity: Penguin, given the Wall Street collapse, should have cut the budget 15%. The National Education Associated (NEA) has co-opted Albany, and most people know it. New York, primarily due to its exorbitant property tax (used to fund the schools) is losing population daily and is about to become the 3rd most populous state after Florida. Does anyone care?

All of these issues lead me to think that many teachers and staff here, especially Mrs. Mrs. Ostrich and Penguin, are more interested in their pay, health benefits, pension, and stature, than in their getting a job done. Most reformers are always ignored, so this neglectful treatment is no surprise to us.

Sincerely,

Dominic Martin

July 14, 2009

Dr. Richard Mills
Commissioner of Education
New York State Education Department
89 Washington Avenue
Albany, NY 12234

Dear Dr. Mills,

When our daughter entered Toad
Lagoon High School in the Fall of 2007,
she had a right to expect a violence-free
school, on full of learning and enthusiasm.
Instead, because of a lack of discipline,
she did not see that sort of atmosphere;
but rather, she was subjected to three
incidents of bullying and hazing. Indeed,
three times we had to go to the police,
not that they really wanted to see us.

We have complained all the way up
the ladder to say one thing: Discipline
at the school is very poor. Do you know
about the illegal class party where hard
liquor was consumed? Do you know
that cellphones are commonly used in
the school during school hours? Do you
know that smoking is tolerated just off
the school grounds? Do you know that
drugs are often dealt from the 2nd floor
lockers? Do you know that our daughter
was slugged at 8am in a classroom after

she had only been in school for 1/1/2 months?

Mr. Daily's recent note says that all is fine when, clearly, it is not. What about our daughter who has had a terrible experience: Was she not due more than this? She recently took her Regents' Exams at the library, so great is her fear of some classmates within the school doing something violent to her.

I think that the two administrator here, Penguin and Mrs. Ostrich, are more interested in keeping their jobs than in doing them. I believe that the "Safe School Team" is a rubber-stamp, not an objective tribunal. And, since you are the head leader of a long list of people who still ignore this issue, we hold you responsible for their inaction and inattention; and also for Emily's disastrous two years spent at the school. Is that the legacy you wish to leave? Can't we do better than this, for the sake of our children, and learning?

Sincerely,

Dominic Martin

Letter to the Editor

9/2/2009
Mr. Dan McClelland, Editor
Toad Lagoon Free Press
136 Park Street
Toad Lagoon, NY 12986

Dear Mr. Dan McClelland, Editor:

Though not a scientific study, over the years I have noticed an upsetting pattern regarding school hiring: Why is it that disproportionate (and illegal?) preference seems to be given only to those who have happily lived here throughout their lives? Why are next-of-kin, or friends of past hires, so often chosen instead of someone else from outside who may have greater skills or drive? One must ask: Is this obvious nepotism not a clever form of corrupt manipulation by those who run the school whereby they, after achieving these ingratiations, always gain more power? It is a consolidation of a false and fragile wealth, one soon to be dismembered, or so one must hope.

Sincerely,

Dominic Martin

September 5, 2009

Superintendent Seth Penguin:
Toad Lagoon High School
294 Hosley Avenue
Toad Lagoon, NY 12986

Dear Superintendent Penguin,

On his first day of school, after being on the middle/high school campus for 6 or 7 hours, our son, Edward, was approached by a fellow student, she asking him, "Do you smoke marijuana?" I believe she was an upperclassman on the cross-country team. This short story points to the fact that the zero tolerance policy for drugs is a joke. Or, put another way, yet another indication that discipline at the school is pretty poor. Thank you, Bradley.

Sincerely,

Dominic Martin

October 7, 2009
Superintendent Seth Penguin:
Toad Lagoon High School
294 Hosley Avenue
Toad Lagoon, NY 12986

Dear Superintendent Penguin,

Once again, due to the pitiful lack of discipline at the high school, one of our children is being bullied and harassed. _____ and _____, two fellow teammate on the football team have indirectly threatened to beat up our son, after today's game. Since the principal is an OSTRICH, I am writing to you as well as the District Attorney and the Stat's Director of Education; and the Safe School Team.

Should something unfortunate befall my boy today, say, that he happens to fall down coming out of the locker room and hit his head or break his arm, I will hold you personally responsible. I have advised him too, that if he ever feels personally threatened in any way, and because of the many weeks of constant verbal abuse that he has already received, that he has every right to defend himself and that he is to do so most vigorously.

Why don't you stop swanning around and run your school like a man?

Sincerely,

Dominic Martin

cc: Darryl L. Daily (Safe School Team of NY State)
        Derek Champagne

October 29, 2009

Dr. David M. Steiner
Commissioner of Education
New York State Education Department
89 Washington Avenue
Albany, NY 12234

Dear Commissioner David Steiner:

Mrs. Ostrich and Superintendent Penguin ought to be fired. We have fought this bullying and hazing for over 2 years. We have a file on the Toad Lagoon High School as thick as a phone book. We do not want <u>anyone</u> hurt. Currently there is neither the desire nor the means to <u>compel</u> <u>obedience</u>.

Daily should probably go as well, since he is a mere "rubber-stamp." Lassitude reigns; given what we spend in these schools, pitiful. Please help.

Sincerely,

Dominic Martin

October 29, 2009
Superintendent Seth Penguin:
Toad Lagoon High School
294 Hosley Avenue
Toad Lagoon, NY 12986

Darryl L. Daily
New York State Education Department
Safe Schools and Alternative Education
Team
89 Washington Avenue
Albany, New York 12234

Dear Superintendent Penguin and Mr. Daily,

Yesterday, October 28, our son Edward was involved, not for the first time, in a shoving match with _____. For years _____ has been saying around Toad Lagoon High School that he wishes to bang our daughter. Also, he tells those that will listen that he wants to sleep with _____. Recently, he has told our son that "your mom sucks penis." This kid is clearly disturbed, ought to be suspended form both the school and the football team; he needs counseling very badly.

Yesterday, he taunted Edward that he is queer (which, thankfully, he is not), and, in the face of this deluge of filth, to avoid being a pansy and as we have instructed him, our son may have been the physical aggressor. I don't care. We will not have our son become a punching bag. Accordingly, I am teaching him how to box. Meanwhile, his grades suffer. Pathetic!

Let us be clear: If some unfortunate accident were to befall our boy, we will hold you both personally responsible. The resultant trial would both hurt your reputation and harm your careers.

Finally, two things remain:

1) There is very little discipline at the school. And

2) The "safe school" program is a joke.

Get to work.

Dominic Martin

P.S. This may be considered a repeat of the _____ fiasco, where you, once again, ignored my advice.

cc: Daily
        D.A. Champagne
        Commissioner of Education
        Steiner
        Toad Lagoon Police Department

November 4, 2009

Dr. David M. Steiner
Commissioner of Education
New York State Education Department
89 Washington Avenue
Albany, NY 12234

Dear Commissioner David Steiner:

For the past two years, as parents, we have been fighting the bullying and hazing, the pornographic language and the pervasive lack of discipline at the Toad Lagoon High School, yet, despite those efforts and the good intentions of some of the staff, bad behavior on the part of far too many of the students continues.

I note that the President Obama's new Secretary of Education is forming a new, nationwide task force to combat this runaway problem. But let me say one thing on this issue: If we wish to solve the problem (and not just convene silly meetings full of useless talk), only two courses of action much be followed:

1) Ban cellphones from all high school campuses. Kids text each other while "studying." Bring back the old pay phone to schools. Supply the quarters.

2) Reinstate some judicious and controlled corporal punishment. The occasional bad kid must be compelled

to obey, something which will only take place if he is slightly afraid, slightly intimidated. As George Washington said: "All Life is Force."

Unless there 2 simple measures are followed, the lack of discipline will only grow. Yes, the ACLU will fight these measures and some teachers will moan, but, so what? Many of today's students, far too many, have little or no respect for authority, and that means that once they get out in the workforce, where they perhaps will have a <u>boss</u> <u>who</u> <u>barks</u>, maybe someone like me, that they will be unprepared.

To repeat, the question is only this: How does a teacher or administrator compel the odd, or common, bad kid to obey? I just gave to you two tools. Funny how that word: Obey, is today so infrequently said. That is because now, with the complete breakdown of the hierarchy, bad kids run the show, or the foxes mind the chicken coop. It is past time for the schools to <u>take</u> <u>back</u>.

By the way? Mrs. Ostrich and Superintendent Penguin should both go. They do not show a clear inclination to do the job.

Sincerely,

Dominic Martin

Darryl L. Daily
The State Education Department / The
University of the State of New York
Albany, NY 12234

November 9, 2009

Dominic & Catherine Martin
334 State Route 421
Toad Lagoon, New York 12986

Dear Mr. and Mrs. Martin:

I have been requested to respond to your October 29, 2009 letter. In your letter to Commissioner Steiner you mentioned that your son is being subjected to bullying and harassment by a particular student at the Toad Lagoon High School in Toad Lagoon, New York. You also mentioned that in previous correspondences, and this one, the school has not responded to the needs of both your daughter and now your son in regards to being bullied and harassed.

In response to your most recent letter, it is suggested that you first try to make contact and request a meeting with the Principal to discuss your concerns and what the school has planned for the safety and academic needs of your 'son within the school. During the meeting you could request for the school to provide a written safety plan in writing to address his concerns with this other student. If the meeting is unsuccessful, a second suggestion is to establish contact with the Superintendent and request a meeting to further investigate as to what plans the school would have in place to address your son's needs and concerns as a result of the other students continuously harassing your son. Again, you could request in writing a response as to what the school is going to do to address this particular situation. A third suggestion would be to address the Board of Education to look into the situation further as it relates to your son. A fourth proactive suggestion would be to become actively involved on the Safety Committee where you could help with the establishment of a Code of Conduct that is fair and equitable for all students within the building and ensure the safety of each child in the school. Each correspondence and meeting with school officials should be documented and a request for follow up is encouraged as you continue to move forward with trying to resolve this problem.

It is suggested that as you try to resolve the issues and communicate with the school district and you try to refrain from opinions of individuals and use factual information as you move forward in your communication and correspondences and look for resolution.

Thank you for your concern with the safety of our children in New York State. If you have any further questions or concerns, you can contact me at (518) 486-6090 or DDAILY@MAIL.NYSED.GOV.

Sincerely,

Darryl Daily

November 17, 2009

Darryl L. Daily
New York State Education Department
Safe Schools and Alternative Education
Team
89 Washington Avenue
Albany, New York 12234

Dear Mr. Daily:

In response to your letter of November 9, I have only one word: Pitiful.

For two years we have fought consistently this issue. Now, our second child is going through the same cruel and unwanted gauntlet. And your weak letter of November 9 is the state's response?

I have not met with the principal, the superintendent and the Board of Education, non of whom seem too troubled by the problem. They lack both the tools and the volition to address the issue. Nearly every day I hear about other kids who are pushed down stairs, tripped up, or insulted. <u>Many</u> parents, like we, are fed up with the lassitude, the foot dragging, and the state's lack of a clear and focused determination to fight the problem.

For months I've heard sexual slurs made by Toad Lagoon miscreants against both my wife and my daughter, who because of your office extreme laziness has had a perfectly disastrous high school experience. I blame you and your crew: Why do you persist in backing the current staff of ostriches, rather than believing parents who hear from their children? I'm telling you flat out: The place has broken down.

By the way, don't tell me to be quiet. We fought world wars in order to secure and protect all American's right to free speech. Do your job!

Sincerely,

Dominic Martin

November 13, 2009

Dr. David M. Steiner
Commissioner of Education
New York State Education Department
89 Washington Avenue
Albany, NY 12234

Dear Commissioner Steiner,

Please see the attached November 11 article in the Toad Lagoon Free Press. I cannot believe my eyes: More self-serving tripe from the lazy and outclassed upper level staff at Toad Lagoon High School. Why don't you ask Mrs. Ostrich and Superintendent Penguin why so many parents pull their children? Look for honesty and transparency in their answers.

Now, without the proper tools, there is no way for staff to compel a bad student, or a good student doing something bad, to obey.

For them to muscle the local newspaper editor to print this "Cover My Ass" pabulum demonstrates just how tall the grass really is. What a mistake! What an error! I believe, and many, many others in town concur, that these 2 administrators are more interested in their salary, health care package and future pensions plans than anything else.

Sincerely,

Dominic Martin

Article from the Toad Lagoon Free Press, 11/11/09

Heading: Discipline incidents down dramatically now in school

Discipline issues at the Toad Lagoon junior-senior high school have seen a dramatic decline in recent years.

In her report to the board of education, Principal Ostrich produced a compilation of the number of students who were sent to the principal's office or to the office of the dean of students for disciplinary matters and the number of incidents involved for each of the past nine school years.

During the school year 2001-02 when Gene Johnson was principal and Bob Tebo was the discipline officer there were 2,486 incidents of discipline by 312 students.

Three years later when Mrs. Ostrich was in her first year as principal and Rick Cowles was the student discipline officer, there were 2,318 incidents caused by 290 students.

By last year, according to Mrs. Ostrich's numbers, those discipline statistics were a fraction of what they were eight years earlier. Last year (2008-09) the number of discipline incidents totaled 1,296. The number of students involved was only 213.

Within the data there was another good year that was marked with fewer than normal discipline cases. In 2003 and 2004 there were only 1,291 cases—five fewer than last year. The incidents that year, when Principal Johnson and Rick Cowles were in charge, were caused by 247 students.

Since 2006-07 Steve Skiff has been the dean of discipline at the local school. A comparison of the months of only September showed that in the first month of the school year five years ago there were 361 incidents by students requiring disciplinary action. The incidents this past September were about one-eighth of that number—only 51 incidents.

Mrs. Ostrich admitted she and the faculty members at the school were excited by the progress made in recent years curbing discipline issue. The board members have cited concern when the numbers have been released in the past.

"Today we have less disruptions at our school. We have more kids receiving instruction in the classroom than ever before!"

Mrs. Ostrich said this year Mr. Skiff is "handling about 95%" of all discipline cases, "and he's doing a great job with these troubled kids!"

"It's an awesome time to be in our school . . . the kids are learning, the teachers are happy they're teaching" and trouble is on the wane, she told the board members.

Board President Mike Dechene said the situation in 2001—his first year on the school board. "We were shocked when we read the discipline numbers. From that time on, one of the board's primary missions was to come up with various programs to curb discipline issues."

He applauded Mrs. Ostrich's report, adding: "we're definitely doing something right."

Superintendent of Schools Seth Penguin said the improved behavior of middle and high school students during school hours seems to be spilling over into community life. In discussions with village police, he learned that during mischief night several weeks ago there were "zero" cases of trouble associated with local students.

He applauded the efforts of the town recreation department in organizing the middle school dance on the here. Attendance at the dance topped 150 students.

The high attendance at the event was attributed in part to the popularity of the Toad Lagoon band, Abbott Hayes, the five members of which donated their time and musical talents to entertain the kids and keep them off local streets that night.

Another factor in fewer discipline problems at the school is the successful Red Ribbon campaign directed by Substance Abuse Coordinator Brooke Hample, who according to Mrs. Ostrich works "hard to see that students get the instruction they need."

She also noted that during one of the recent Red Ribbon weeks, Toad Lagoon students challenged their peers in Saranac Lake in a contest to see who could collect more food for the local food pantry. Toad Lagoon won the contest.

L.P. Quinn Interim Principal Carolyn Merrihew also applauded Brooke's work, which this year has been expanded to cover students in all grades, from pre-K to 12. "The kids are so motivated by her enthusiasm," the principal told the board.

November 13, 2009

Mr. Dan McClelland, Editor
Toad Lagoon Free Press
136 Park Street
Toad Lagoon, NY 12986

Dear Dan,

I found the recent article on the decrease of disciplinary incidents at the Toad Lagoon High School to be quite misleading. Just because there has been, going back nearly 10 years and covering many different administrations, a reported drop in trouble does not mean that discipline has necessarily improved. Have the standards for what constitutes a disciplinary event remained constant? That is highly unlikely. Indeed, it could mean the opposite: Incidents are intrinsically downplayed or ignored so that, for the lead staff, to the public, they look better, or seem to.

Bullying and hazing continue. Our son was on the high school grounds only 6 hours before he was offered marijuana. As a parent of 2 non-native students there, I will say conclusively that cliques of all sorts abound. And twenty percent (or more) of the students do not graduate making what we are spending on the graduating students, effectively, even more, exorbitant. Does anyone in charge there in Albany wish to examine what is spent now per student, versus, say, 1970?

Here is one way to improve discipline: Get rid of cell phones completely. Students text during class, parents' and teachers' protests notwithstanding. Texting leads to a dearth of learning and abuse of others, especially among the girls. Bring back a bank of pay phones and have the main office put in a large supply of quarters to use them.

I found the article, once again, very self-serving. The quality of the school should not be lamely bolstered by misleading statistics. Why do so many parents pull their kids out of the school? Answer: They are tired of the baloney or, what my father used to call, "hornswoggling."

Sincerely,

Dominic Martin

Letter From Darryl L. Daily
The State Education Department/
University of the State of New York
Albany, NY 12234

November 24, 2009

Dominic & Catherine Martin
334 State Route # 421
Toad Lagoon, New York 12986

Dear Mr. & Mrs. Martin:

Thank you for sharing your concern with the recent article on disciplinary incidents at Toad Lagoon High School. You expressed in a letter to Commissioner Steiner on November 13, 2009 that there are many parents pulling their children out of the High School due to the lack of discipline within the school. You mentioned that the article from the Toad Lagoon Free Press was written by the editor to cover the administrator's reputations and expressed that the discipline has not improved as a result of their actions. In addition, you offered your opinion on improving discipline at the school.

In our previous correspondences I suggested that you follow the chain of command and keep detailed documentation of your communication with the school district. You followed this guidance as demonstrated in the previous letters you provided. I also suggested that you become involved with the school's Safety Committee. This would allow you to be part of the decision making process and be proactive in developing a Code of Conduct for the school.

Thank you for your concern with the safety of our children in New York State. If you have any further questions or concerns, you can contact me at (518) 473-1233 or Ddaily@mail.nysed.gov.

Respectfully,

Darryl Daily
Assistant in Education
Improvement Services

Email to: Dominic Martin

From: Darryl L. Daily
New York State Education Department

Dated: November 24, 2009

Dear Mr. Martin,

Thank you for sharing the concern for your son being harassed at Toad Lagoon High School in Toad Lagoon, New York. You expressed in a letter to me dated 11/17/09 that you are blaming the school for your son's experiences of continued harassment while in attendance at the school. It is unfortunate we offered the proper process to follow and you have not been satisfied with the result. If still you are not pleased with the school's decisions on discipline you and other concerned parents could establish on the agenda for the Board of Education to address the issues that they share.

If still the situation is widespread you and your neighbors select the school board members that effect the decisions that are made in the school. You could exercise your right to vote new members to the board that represent your views. In addition, you have the right to remove your son as a student from this school to another school.

If you have any further questions or concerns, you can contact me at the numbers provided below:

Respectfully,

Darryl L. Daily
New York State Education Department
Safe Schools and Alternative Education Team
89 Washington Avenue
Room 318 M-EB
Albany, New York 12234
Office: (518) 486-3640
Direct Line: (518) 473-1233
Cell: (518) 330-5722
DDAILY@MAIL.NYSED.GOV
Fax: (518) 474-8299
http://www.emsc.nysed.gov/ssae/

Official Complaint Filed with New York State Education Department:

December 4, 2009

1. Describe the concerns that led you to file this complaint. Be sure to include all important information including the date of the alleged incident.

For approximately 6 weeks various classmates including _____ and _____ have been harassing our son Edward. The comments include: "You're a fag," "You like men," "I want to bang your mom," I want to bang your sister," etc. Understandably, because of these comments, pushing and shoving have started, and some punches have been thrown.

Yesterday, _____ punched _____'s head into a cement block wall while he was getting a drink. I have told our son that if he is pushed or punched or shoved to retaliate with a vengeance. Accordingly, I have been teaching him how to defend himself and how to box. This is our second child to go to this very bad school. Our older daughter _____ went through much of the same.

2. State your proposed resolution of the problem. State what you would suggest NYSED do to resolve this issue.

We have complained to the board, the principal and the superintendent but to no avail. I must say that Mr. John Butler, the A.D., has tried mightily to help solve the problem. But, here is the basic issue: The school lacks discipline. The students do not respect authority.

Though cell phones are banned, they are used <u>routinely</u>. I have heard from our daughter that drugs are sold from the second floor lockers. At dismissal, rarely are any teachers present to project authority and to make sure that the kids do not do something wrong. A month ago, I saw a student at dismissal with his pants down around his ankles, entertaining the crowd. Both the principal and the superintendent refuse to dig in and solve the problem and, therefore, they should both be moved aside and teachers who are <u>not</u> <u>outsiders</u> hired. Many teachers agree with these points but do not wish to speak out since they are correctly afraid of losing their jobs. The students are running the system. Last spring, for example, as part of Senior Skip Day, the seniors had a very long, late-night party at which hard alcohol was consumed. Mrs. Ostrich and Superintendent Penguin should be stopped this party. We are looking at all alternatives so that our <u>second</u> child does not have to go to this bad school. Please help. <u>Many</u> <u>other</u> parents believe as we do.

December 13, 2009

Darryl L. Daily
New York State Education Department
Safe Schools and Alternative Education
Team
89 Washington Avenue
Albany, New York 12234

Dear Mr. Daily:

This past Friday night, our daughter, received a voice mail probably from one of her prior classmates calling her, for probably the 100th time, a "slut." Do you understand what this has done to our daughter? There is only one thing which work: Ban cell phones from all high schools! They are used as weapons, and function just like a gun or bomb. Any other response will not work, and, therefore, is a waste of time.

Sincerely,

Dominic Martin

December 15, 2009

Darryl L. Daily
New York State Education Department
Safe Schools and Alternative Education
Team
89 Washington Avenue
Albany, New York 12234

Dear Mr. Daily,

Yesterday afternoon, as he was leaving Toad Lagoon High School, our son, Edward Martin, standing at the top of a flight of concrete stairs, was pushed from behind. A shoving match/fight ensued. Clearly, there is little respect for authority in that school. Every day we fear for our son's safety and emotional health. Mr. John Bean, A.D., is trying to help; others—I am not so sure. I may write a book on this issue entitled: Saint Joseph Has Lost His Hammer: Bullying and Hazing Has Swamped Our Nation's Schools and How to Stop It.

Sincerely,

Dominic Martin

Spring 2010
Heading: Mickey Mantle, Maury Wills, Jim Gilliam; not the first one, but the second and the last
An email to two coaches at the Toad Lagoon High School:

I was very disappointed to hear that you had prohibited our son, Edward, from hitting left-handed. For nearly ten years I have coached him to be a switch-hitter. Why, just this past weekend, batting left-handed against a former Yankee pitching prospect (now old like us), he smartly slashed a liner down the right-field line. Since he clearly has this talent, I fail to see the harm.

Secondly, I am very unhappy that you kicked him off the team. For this entire school year and probably because he is "not from town", Edward has been kidded, chided, made fun of, pushed, shoved—you name it. Doubtless, he is not an innocent. Sometimes, he should have walked away from a fight. But I do not wish our son to be a punching bag; yet sometimes Lucian, a contest cannot be postponed. Knowing that he was not from town, not part of the pack of undisciplined, myopic marauders, perhaps you could have done more, both to protect him and to foster team cohesiveness. Your solution was incorrect, and serves to confirm to the marauders that they can do whatever they want.

Dominic Martin

Letter to the Editor, Toad Lagoon Free Press

June 7, 2010

Mr. Dan McClelland, Editor
Toad Lagoon Free Press
136 Park Street
Toad Lagoon, NY 12986

Dear Editor Dan McClelland,

The consternation occasioned by public school teacher layoffs is predictable: Too many teachers were hired in the first place! Operating under the mistaken idea that education automatically improves the way more public funds are spent, goaded into new educational programs by an always thirsty NEA, squeezed by a corrupt state government wherein backroom deals are the norm, local districts wonder what happened. Only one proper analysis pertains: What did we spend on education, per student and corrected for inflation, in 1970 and how did those students fare, both in school and in life, and how does that number compare to today's? One must not forget to factor in today's much higher dropout rate to get a true comparison.

For years, Toad Lagoon, and many towns like it, has had too many public sector jobs. With the death of the mills this was bound to happen. The problem is this: When schools are mostly funded by property tax revenues, that burden places an unfair and untenable load on the homeowners. Excessive school spending across the nation is slowly billing the idea of home ownership. The thirst for knowledge is mostly self-generated, engendered by well meaning parents in the home. For schools to try to supplant the role of two parents, as is now practiced, is folly.

Sincerely,

Dominic Martin

June 9, 2010

Dr. David M. Steiner
Commissioner of Education
New York State Education Department
89 Washington Avenue
Albany, NY 12234

Dear Dr. Steiner:

I hope you recall our family since for nearly three years out two eldest children have had to endure the vilest abuse, the most disgusting taunts at that unpolished sanitarium which passes for a high school in Toad Lagoon. Just today, our son, Edward, aged 13, read in the school's bathroom mirror that he was a queer. (Thankfully, he is not.) One of the teachers, a Mrs. Staves, must have been surprised to learn that she sports a penis. And on and on.

There is precious little discipline at the school. The two main administrators, Mrs. Ostrich and Superintendent Penguin, have shown a distinct disinterest in tackling the problem. Lassitude reigns; and your office, it seems, is more interested in protecting those "already in the club," rather than the younger students who are at a precarious point in their lives. Some good teachers do work there, but they are intimidated by

Penguin's threats of reprisals: And who wants to lose his job now? But, is this the best we can do?

As it is, Toad Lagoon High School is a disaster. Many parents have yanked their children out, tired of the bullying Penguin, the ineffectual Mrs. Ostrich, and the constant abuse thrust upon their children. I do not know if you are a father, but if you are, how would you like to hear that your son sucks penis, or that your daughter is a slut? All of this and more we have had to endure.

We have written a book describing all this, and it is called St. Joseph Has Lost His Hammer: How Bullying and Hazing Has Swamped our Schools and How to Fix It. It is now at my typist's office for inclusion on a disc soon to be sent to iUniverse at which point it will be available for purchase. Soon, the whole ugly story will be told: The evasions, the lassitude, the lack of responsibility taken. Soon, you will all be famous, but for the wrong reasons.

Sincerely,

Dominic Martin

Letter from The State Education
Department / The University of the State
of New York

June 23, 2010

Dominic Martin
PO Box 95
McFarland, KS 66501

Mr. Martin,

Your letter has been forwarded to me
for a response. I would like to thank you
for taking the time to write to the New
York State Education Department.

In reading your letter it appears
you have a few concerns regarding your
children's high school. Bullying is a very
serious matter. The link below, along with
your own district's policy on bullying,
may provide you with information
needed to help address the problem
area. http://www.emsc.nysed.gov/ssae/
schoolsafely/sdfsca/bullying html

If you have concerns regarding the
behavior of a school administrator,
faculty member, and/or staff person, you
have the right to an appeal through the
education system. You would begin with a
letter of complaint to the Principal, then a
letter to the Superintendent followed by,
a letter to the Local Board of Education

(BOE) and finally to the New York State Commissioner of Education. You cannot appeal directly to the Commissioner without first exhausting the local appeal system as noted above.

Instructions for making an appeal to the Commissioner of Education can be obtained at www.counsel.nysed.gov. This site also maintains copies of all the judicial decisions rendered by the Commissioner of Education.

Should you have further questions, I can be reached at (518) 486-6090.

Sincerely.

Audrey Almela
Assistant in Education
Improvement Services

July 9, 2010

Audrey Almela
Assistant in Education Improvement
Services
The State Education Department / The
University of the State of New York
Office of Student Support Services
89 Washington Ave., Room 318M EB
Albany, New York 12234

Dear Ms. Almela,

I need more hoops to jump through!
Please, give me more hoops! Ha!

Why should parents who have
seen what we have seen happen to our
children have to beg for your attention?

Answer: Everyone not a teacher nor
an administrator knows that your ilk
principally protects their own, thinking
that the general citizens can go hang.

Dominic Martin

July 9, 2010

Dr. David M. Steiner
Commissioner of Education
New York State Education Department
89 Washington Ave
Albany, NY 12234

Dear Commissioner Steiner,

I wanted you to see this pitiful letter from Ms. Almela. After all that our family has been through for three years, her weak response is laughable.

The issue is this: What kind of leadership from you may we expect? What sort of person rises to the top? Is the Peter Principle at work wherein leaders, such as yourself, mostly protect their own, always circling the wagons, and never admitting mistakes or errors in judgment?

By the way, my wife tells me that 10 more students are leaving Toad Lagoon High School for Long Lake, their parents apparently as tired of the lack of discipline as we are.

Between your bureaucracy and we parents, very little proper communication exists, not from our want of trying. I am reminded of Harry Truman's belief in his responsibility to his constituents: "I have always believed that if a person goes to the trouble of writing a letter, even a critical letter, I should answer or at least acknowledge it." How the world has changed!

Meanwhile, the book, St. Joseph Has Lost His Hammer, goes to the printer. As I travel and move about, I mention it to dozens of people and nearly all are alarmed both to the extent of the problem and at the state's ineffectual response. It is a nationwide dilemma which only grows worse. And to think: Your office could have taken a strong lead in defeating it.

Dominic Martin

p.s. I wonder, did you not see the growing problem? Did you not wish to grapple with it? Have you not seen the possibility there to achieve greatness, if you subdued this menace? Did any of this occur to you or were you just a policy wonk, content with studies, pleased with colloquia? Preferably, that greatness would have been unrecognized; yet, for the kids you would have done some good.

Letter from The State Education Department / The University of the State of New York

July 30, 2010

Mr. Dominic Martin
P.O. Box 95
McFarland, KS 66501
Dear Mr. Martin:

I am in receipt of your letters to Commissioner of Education David Steiner, dated June 9, 2010, the response to that letter from Audrey Almela, dated June 23, 2010 and separate letters to Dr. Steiner and Ms. Almela which are both dated July 9, 2010 concerning the mistreatment of your family, particularly of your son Edward at the Toad Lagoon Central School District. I have been asked to respond to your correspondence as the senior professional at the Education Department who advises schools and families concerning student behaviors and school policies that create barriers to learning within the areas of attendance and discipline.

Based upon your request for the assistance, I would like to talk with you about these issues and the options available to you. I believe that a dialogue between us provides a greater potential for understanding the options available to you than anything that I could write in the same period of time. I can be reached Monday through Friday from 9:00 AM to 5:00 PM at 518-486-6090. If I am away from my desk or on the phone, I will call you back if you leave your telephone number. I look forward to talking with you.

Sincerely,

Carl N. Friedman

August 25, 2010
Mr. Carl Friedman
Safe School Team
New York State Education Department
89 Washington Avenue
Albany, New York 12234

Dear Mr. Friedman:

No. I do not wish to speak with you. For nearly three years, since November of '07 when our daughter was involved in a fistfight in the classroom, our family has been ignored, mocked, avoided, and intimidated. I see no purpose to a conversation.

Superintendent Penguin in the period of time called me once to yell at me and deride my points. Within the same time frame, Mrs. Ostrich left one brief message. So much for an alert leadership. So much for grappling with a problem. So much for not giving up till the battle is done, and won.

Clearly, as our book proves, the will to win does not exist. What we have constantly heard is that bullying and hazing is a difficult problem. Not good enough when your child's adolescence is at stake. Two of our children suffered at that terrible school, one led (if that is the word) by administrators more interested in their big paychecks and pensions than in helping the kids.

Further, as my book proves, the state's bureaucracy is a joke. Mostly, they circle the wagons and defend themselves against all charges, however correct. All involved, through the inability to grapple and fix the problem, deserve the most serious charge: Corrupt. For, to take money and <u>not</u> fix the problem is the essence of corruption.

Dominic Martin

p.s. The book is out soon. <u>You</u> <u>all</u> are in it!

August 25, 2010

District Attorney Derek P. Champagne
355 West Main Street
Malone, NY 12953

Dear D.A. Derek Champagne:

Yesterday our son, Edward Martin, now living in McFarland, KS where I've taken a teaching position, received an intimidating phone call from some of the same morons who bullied him last year at Toad Lagoon High School, they saying to him: "Did you order an extra-large penis?" My wife and I have witnessed this kind of junk for three years. The morons fear no one since they know that there will never be, from that listless school, any retribution. Accordingly, you may want to consider additional, new statutes expressly directed towards stopping juvenile hi-tech bullying. Don't you wish to help?

Sincerely,

Dominic Martin

August 26, 2010

Mr. Carl Friedman
Safe School Team
New York State Education Department
89 Washington Avenue
Albany, New York 12234

Dear Mr. Friedman,

You should know that just yesterday, our son, Edward Martin, even though now living with me in Kansas, received a salacious, bullying phone call from some of the same unpunished morons who taunted him last year at Toad Lagoon High School, they saying to him: "Did you order an extra-large penis?" This is further proof that TLHS is in serious trouble. Do you not believe me? For three years do you think we have been making this junk up? What if it were your son, your daughter?

But, no matter; soon, our book, <u>St. Joseph Has Lost His Hammer</u>, will shortly be published and people all over the state will then be able to see the bungling ineptitude, the passivity, the constant shirking of responsibility, the corruption, the will to win: To combat and vanquish this epidemic, is nonexistent.

Sincerely,

Dominic Martin

August 26, 2010

Mr. Dan McClelland, Editor
Toad Lagoon Free Press
136 Park Street
Toad Lagoon, NY 12986
Dear Dan McClelland,

On August 25, our son received a crude and senseless phone call from some of the same unpunished morons who bullied him last year at Toad Lagoon High School, even though he now lives 1600 miles away. Thus, the bullying continues. I will not say what he was told since it does not befit a family newspaper. Why should children or teenagers have to grow up in such a tainted, hateful environment? As we have seen, this kind of thing is expected at the school and routinely goes unpunished; the school staff does nothing, saying only, "It is a difficult problem." Foxhole Normans" all, nobody wants to act, or can.

We have: We have written a book about the bungling ineptitude at the school; it is entitled St. Joseph Has Lost His Hammer. All the laziness, all the listlessness, all the shirking of responsibility is laid bare.
Sincerely,

Dominic Martin

Popularity is key to a good high school experience. This is one of the most common misconceptions to have when entering high school but sadly is true. Without popularity students sometimes feel that they are being bullied and the fighting takes control. These days many teachers do not handle it the way they should and do not take any actions such as not providing a stricter punishment guideline and other options that can help put a stop to the many students who are getting away with it. This has not only forced an abundant amount of students to change who they are to fit in but cost a good amount of them in America their happiness and their lives.

Many teens attending a high school have now started changing who they are on the outside just to become considered into the "in" category of the social popularity level. By doing this they choose to give up their kindness and friendship to those whom are not in the "cool" crowd and thus make them feel rejected. They do this to prevent being put down by their "popular" friends and back into the "unpopular" group. Movies such as Mean Girls show people everywhere the kind of social system that goes in all over the country we live in. The problem proven here is the lack of authority within the teachers and discipline towards the students.

Years ago when I had gone to school in England and attended a preparatory school, discipline and respect was a very strong aspect in making the school run appropriately. As students we had to follow the rules or suffer the consequences. We wore uniforms to show ourselves as equals: not based on our family's money and also had to rise to our feet whenever the headmaster entered each of our classrooms. If we misbehaved we risked our individual sports programs and sometimes it could even be as bad leading to being expelled. Even though our discipline and authority by the teachers may seem harsh but it made us strong, smart, and respectful of others especially elders leaving play time to the playground whilst still remaining in a fun and learning environment.

To all of the students who were not embraced with a school like the one I attended, I would encourage them to always be true to themselves and be respectful of others no matter what type of school they attend. School is a learning center for everyone and should be treated as one. Be true to others and you will be true to yourself and if someone is not acting as a friend should be and is happy chasing for popularity then they may not be a friend worth crying over.

Emily Martin

Hello future signer with the Yankees,

This is me, talking to myself in the future, it will be five years until I and you will read this. This is what happened in 7th grade. I thought that I would write it down so that it was not forgotten. Not that I could ever forget 7th grade. I had moved up to the Middle/High School from LP Quinn. So, here are the highlights:

Sports

Sports have always kept me going. Right now when I grow up, I want to play for the New York Yankees. People tell me I won't, but I tell them about Babe Ruth, and Derek Jeter. People told them they won't play for the Yankees, but now they are perhaps the greatest players of all time. I also tell them that their goal in life is to put people down and tell them not to chase their dreams—they are all jerks!!!

Last November, the Yankees won their 27th championship in their own new stadium. When I watched it happen, I cried because I was so overjoyed. I want to be like that. To make it there, I will work extra hard, and try to ignore the put-downs. I was on the basketball team. I was okay, but not great, even though I wanted to be like Larry Bird or

Magic Johnson. At the end of the season, they wouldn't let me play because of my inadequate grades. Then I couldn't practice. It was really dumb.

In football, I tried my best to be the best. People made fun of me constantly because I wanted to go to Notre Dame and then go play for the Yankees. ON MY VERY OWN TEAM!!!!!!! They wouldn't let me play that much. Not just me, some other players too. My assistant coach was my mentor, pushing us until the last yard; he always used to say "Drive till the whistle". That inspired me. His name was Coach Cochran, but it was really Doug Cochran. I believe he was my real coach. Our main coach to me, wasn't a real coach, he never pushed us. He just stood there and did nothing, just toss the football up and down. His name was Mr. Tower. He almost made it o the majors but was cut because he hurt his shoulder. He never made it to the majors, but pitched in the minors.

In baseball, I felt great, it is my favorite sport. My coaches were Mr. Bartlett and Mr. Pickering. I was hitting my best. When my Dad talked to our main coach, Mr. Bartlett, he barely even talked to him, this happened to all my coaches. Something weird about that, huh? My assistant coaches were the real coaches, they were all good men. They went to practice on time and helped us to improve. I liked that. All my assistant coaches really pushed us. One day in practice when we were playing infield outfield, I was in left field along with Dylan Lohr. Instead of hitting it to me, Coach Bartlett just skipped me and went on to center field. I waited until it came back to me. I was in a ready stance, eyes poised just waiting fof the ball to be hit to me and then throw it to second. That didn't go along with my plan. He just looked at me for about 10 seconds. Then he yelled at me and told Dylan to get in. When I got kicked off, I was happy about that. The reason I got kicked off baseball was because I got in a fight with Jeremy Suave. He was throwing baseballs at me, pretty hard too. So I returned fire and threw some back. He then tackled me. It was bad. I was just protecting myself, like my for fathers. To tell you the truth, Mitch Kenniston, and Kevin Becker (my best friends) I highly respected, they were the only ones who stood up for me. That's practically it from sports.

School

To tell you the truth, school hasn't been great this year. Some teachers never try to encourage you for success. The only teacher I highly respected was Mr.

McIntosh. He always helped me. He was a good man and a good teacher. It would be a huge and I mean HUGE mistake to fire him. My other teachers, from my perspective, were only interested in the paycheck. They didn't care about us. Mrs. Mitchell, every day, when we didn't do something good on a test or report, she would practically call us all dumb. Good teachers would encourage us for success. She said I had an attitude. Well yes, I did. Why? Because I was made about what she said to us. She deserves to be fired. I never got the reason she said I had an attitude. It was pretty messed up.

Friends

Well, 2009-2010, wasn't a real good thing with friends. People bullied me constantly. They were such jerks. Well, I made it. That's the good thing. No phone calls to come hang out or for a sleepover either! Except Kevin on his birthday. Which we stayed up all night and played fall out three. Hahaha, such good times. Well, it was a great year. I had quite a lot of fun. This year went really fast. We had our disappointments and ours successes. We helped each other. But sometimes people aren't like that. Friends are the ones who help you and encourage you. You need friends.

The U.S. Military

I love the military. The people who are in it are brave and are doing it for other people they know nothing about. My family is a military family. Practically every single family member has been in the military. On Memorial Day I got to play for veterans on my alto sax. Hopefully in the future, Americans will finally realize what the military had done for us.

Music

I liked a lot of different music this year. From rap to rock. I've liked many bands this year. Like Slipknot, Lil Wayne, Linkin Park, Eminem, Train, Ludacris, 50 cent and more. I love music. I play in the middle school band. I play the alto sax. Trying not to brag, but I'm pretty good. I've been playing since 4th grade. I actually started off with the tenor sax, but, I wanted to follow in my father and grandfather's path and play the alto. My grandfather actually had a band. He was a very good player. He traveled the world.

Dirt biking

Well it's been since May 2009 that I have had a love for motor sports. I've crashed a lot. But I've gotten back up. I have a dirt bike myself, but it's a piece of crap. But I'll get a new one for Christmas. I am quite good. I get many of dirt bike tricks from the shown on MTV "Nitro Circus". It's a good show and the host of the show is Travis Pastrana, an amazing dirt biker and is very good at anything.

The New York Yankees

Well, I have a huge obsession with the New York Yankees. I watch every single game. My favorite players are Derek Jeter, and Mark Teixeira. They are all great players. I think they are the best. When I grow up I want to play for them. They have won 27 championships. In my room I have an autographed picture of Mickey Mantle and Joe DiMaggio. I have an autographed picture of Yogi Berra. I have an autographed picture of the great pitcher Lee Smith; I met him when I got it signed. That's all from the New York Yankees.

Notre Dame

After I finish high school, I'm planning on going to Notre Dame. I'm planning on playing football there and be and all American and win the Heisman Trophy Award. People tell me I won't.

They movie, "Rudy", is inspiring me to try to go to Notre Dame. After football, I plan on going to sign up for baseball, get a Yankee scout to see me and decide if I will play for them. I believe that Notre Dame is a special place.

That is what is going on in 7th grade and what went on. As you can see, life has its ups and downs. But I know how to get out of them. Hopefully the things that I don't like will be gone by the time I'm a senior. Remember this, as Coach Cochran said, "Drive till the whistle".

Well that's it from me, friend.
See Ya,

Edward Martin

Chapter Three: Rule the Roast

Rule the Roast: To have the chief direction; to be paramount.

> The phrase was common in the 15th Century and it is possible that <u>roast</u> was originally <u>roost</u>, the reference being to a cock, who decides which hen is to roost nearest him; but in Thomas Heywood's <u>History</u> <u>of</u> <u>Women</u> ©. 1630) we read of "her that ruled the roast in the kitchen".

"Suffolk, the new-made duke that rules the roast."

Shakespeare, <u>Henry</u> <u>VI</u>, Part II (I,i,107) from <u>Brewer's</u> p. 954

This famous phrase, "Rule the Roost," was selected since it brings up the question: Who is in charge? Who runs the show? Not just in terms of the student-teacher dialectic, but, also, secondarily, pointing to this question: Why can't American parents demand and receive better schools, ones with absolutely no bullying and hazing? Is that not the most normal and proper of wishes?

As you have seen, we have been, like most parents, vigilant and undeterred, but also, considerably ignored. Chapter Two has proven that. We were told to "put up with." The problem endures, if it is not, indeed, getting worse, abetted by sequestered, aloof administrators who routinely eschew the difficult.

By the way, I apologize for the occasionally strident tone to some of the letters in "Rough and Ready". I will defend myself (breaking one of Seneca's most important dicta) by saying how personally and quickly any concerned parent reacts when he witnesses a constant, filthy attack on his progeny. The reaction is instantaneous and visceral, emanating from a deep source within one's genetics. It is only instinct, pure and simple.

So, the bullying and hazing continue all across our country. Yet, it should not be tolerated in the least, begging my question: Do we want to stop it? The unacceptable situation reminds me of the flight of Dr. Joseph Mengele, the "Angel of Death", so named for his hideous experiments on prisoners at Auschwitz. After the war, in April of 1945 (that most pivotal of months, witnessing

1) the death of Franklin Roosevelt
2) the sacking of Berlin by the Russians
3) the passivity or paralysis of American troops just 70 miles to the west of Berlin

4) the suicide of Hitler) <u>how</u> did he escape to South America? His son, Rolf, says, "If they really wanted to get him, they could have."[2]

Readers may gauge for themselves how far we, as parents, have gotten with all our impugning remonstrations: Nowhere, or so it seems. It appears that the league of educators is intractable and quite slow on regeneration. Despite our numerous, cogent, and, in most cases, restrained protests, we have been largely ignored, and thus, they and the students rule the roast.

The state bureaucracy of education, employing thousands of highly paid citizens and occupying an enormous building in Albany (The astute president of the college where I worked once, pointedly, asked me: "What do they do in that giant place?"), as far as I know, has done very little. The Commissioner of Education <u>never</u> wrote or called. The "Safe School" Director, Mr. Daily, did call and listened to my predictable rant for 30 minutes, but his letters to us are predictable pap and any actions not apparent. Everyone is afraid to touch the toe to the lake! As stated, Superintendent Penguin did call once, and we interrupted and yelled at each other for a brief time. Mrs. Ostrich called once in 3 years and left a very short message. We have received not one written word from the local school board. Not one teacher has called to offer to us any support, excepting Athletic Director John Bean; thank God for him! Penguin, to coalesce and therefore further strengthen his ascending power, tends to hire only younger, more compliant teachers, who will later tend to be "more beholden" to him in any debate. He does not like independence of thought. He is not the

---

[2] From shop PBS.org, January 2010, p.14

kind of leader who encourages a vigorous debate. And, thus, this conspiracy of silence spreads.

Many excellent teachers work here; however, most of them are afraid to speak up. And who can blame them?: In this resolutely sick economy, who wants to lose his job? And thus the inaction continues, with little benefit to the student.

So, there it is: The entire, sad picture. Paralysis, finger-pointing, evasions and misdirections, sloppiness, and, more than anything else, a colossal lack of will emerge. Some might use that mouthful word: Spinelessness.

Admittedly, the bullying and hazing is a difficult problem. But, faced with that, should one redouble one's effort to combat and eliminate it? When faced with a complex problem, is it proper to give up, to glide along, to accede to the unsuccessful status quo? If faced with difficulties, are we to become slump-shouldered? This is why the failure of the state education bureaucracy is so vexing, so discouraging.

Let me tell to you a story, a story of mice. They were getting into our newly constructed garage. The contractor said, "What do you want? We are in the woods here. They will get in." I answered, "No. Only if you admit that the mice are smarter than you are. And I don't think you want to do that; do you?"

And, over the past three years a couple of kids who had been mean to our kids were briefly suspended, slap-dash, and one fellow was bumped off the football team, though the season was nearly over. The fellow who slashed our daughter's car tire, after many months of opaque denial, finally fessed up. It turns out that that crime had no connection to the nasty and continuing, still, text messaging that she receives. The very active and competent Athletic Director, Mr. John Bean, a number of times has brought our son and various other boys, all with fresh amplitudes of testosterone coursing through their veins and arteries, for:

1) stern,
2) grave,
3) voice-raised,
4) haranguing,
5) vitriolic
6) red-faced,
7) old-fashioned

tongue-lashings, he trying to get all bad behaviors, from whatever boy, to stop; and these conversations, I believe, have done more good than any other factor. He actually gets mad! Can you believe it!

But most teachers refrain. Seeing bad behavior, they ask the teenager to stop it. Ridiculous! Pathetic! What folly! The teenager asks himself: "Shy should I? Where's the penalty?" And he knows that he may do it again and again, since, as I mentioned in Chapter One's "Raven" there is no hammer; St. Joseph has lost it, which bodes us all ill.

But, actually, St. Joseph has not lost it. Being a careful and prudent carpenter, he would, of course, never have lost one of his tools! Rather, society has lost in or, indeed, thrown it away. Any student, contemplating a nefarious act, ought beforehand to say to himself: "If I do that, my life might get ugly, and fast!" Today, more and more, since standards are so loose and so lax and authority so ignored and diminished, that kind of logical mental process often does not take place.

And the results, as Lou Dobbs writes in his excellent book, War as the Middle Class (Penguin Books; New York, 2006) have been beyond disastrous. He writes:

"We've ceded our children's future to the public school system—a faceless bureaucracy that has proven time and time again that it can't change" (pp. 158)

He writes clearly and forcefully in the book, despising all bunk. He believes that we have entered a second generation of failing students. (I agree.) He notes that every year test scores drop or stay flat, despite massive, indeed, skyrocketing spending. In particular, he describes the decline in math and science, studies crucial to those students now in school if after graduation they wish to make a decent living. He basically believes that unless we get serious again, now, today, about education that we will crank out millions of young adults who will not be able to function well in the future and that, for that reason, they will become part of the permanent poor. This sad process has already started! And what a change from, say, 40 years ago when public schools were actually pretty good: Graduates could function in society and school spending was more or less controlled. However, we are talking about a time before the NEA walked into the room, and started to tell everybody what to do.

What is the biggest difference between public high schools of today and when I graduated in 1969? The answer is clear: Discipline has mostly drifted away, abetted by the ACLU—engendered granting of all sorts of ever-expanding rights to the teenager students. Because of that shift, today a teacher can no longer:

1) intimidate
2) scold
3) yell at

4) demean
5) challenge
6) touch in any way
7) scare
8) threaten
9) castigate
10) frighten
11) make timid
12) alarm
13) terrify
14) startle, or you name it.

They may talk and discuss, but only quietly so. We have gone very soft in our approach to discipline, to put it mildly. (Is someone afraid of lawsuits? Probably, but that is another story.) So, once again, absent any of these historic, oft-used tools, that is, not being able to find St. Joseph's missing hammer, how can a teacher compel a misbehaving student to obey? Talk? Discuss? Ask? No. The answer is: He cannot. And, alas, we watch our ruinous and failing schools and see our uninformed and undisciplined students released out into adulthood supremely unequipped for the new world order and its attendant rigor. All the while, the higher-ups will falsely allege that everything is fine but we need just a little more money. Gimmicks! Russels! Cant!

I spent many of my high school years working in orange groves in Southern California. Often my immediate boss was a twentyish ranch foreman who quickly would yell at me whenever I screwed up, which was often, me being a slow 14 year old with wax-laden ears. I learned from this experience two things:

1) My father was not the only man in the world to yell at me.

2) To pay attention to my boss whenever he gave to me an order, and try like hell to carry it out.

Yet, today, because teenagers are often not properly guided or disciplined at home, when they go to high school their primary focus is: "What I want" rather than "What the teacher expects." That is the crux of it, or linchpin. People can no longer take direction anymore since they are not <u>made</u> <u>to</u>. Hierarchies are no longer recognized. One must ask: "Who is in charge?" Who rules the roast? Nobody!

Back in 1965, our family was thinking of moving out of busy and congested Los Angeles to the bucolic orange groves of Ventura County. I was never asked what I thought of that proposed move, nor did I <u>expect</u> to be asked. I was an 8th grader who would move if <u>my parents</u> decided that it was a good idea. How the times have changed!

Later, in 1999, our family was trying to sell our home in the Central Coast of California. A mother came by to look at it, accompanied by her two small sons, aged, say, 6 and 8. She said that she liked our place but would have to ask <u>her</u> <u>sons</u> for their opinion. I was floored. <u>Ancora</u>, <u>I tempi</u> <u>cambiano</u>! *Again, how the times have changed!*

Some will say: One must move with the times, <u>tempori</u> <u>parendum</u> for those who miss the Latin. But, have not all these experiments:

1) the elimination of hierarchies
2) the granting of adult-style rights to teenagers
3) the abolition of any physicality
4) the extinction of orders, or
5) the focus, always, on what a high-schooler feels

resulted in lost students, unfocused and unguided plebs, many of them, driven largely by constantly fluctuating desires? What is the place of the intellect in today's world? That question has been forgotten since educators so strongly desire to be current. Yet, the question is not a curly one.

Instead, teachers never threaten a student with suspension or expulsion like Fr. Nidorf did every day at Villanova back in 1965. (The Dodgers had the Davis brothers, Maury Wills was stealing bases like a whirling dervish and Sandy Koufax's left elbow had not yet gone bluey, the slang word for lead, <u>Brewer's</u>, p. 134). Rather, today, expulsions are rare, even when deserved, because schools are reimbursed based upon enrollment, and most principals do not want a school to function with decreased revenue. Doubtless, this payment system is corrupt.

Further, grade inflation has made graduation, and before that, the honor roll, a mockery. Whoever invented the "A+" grade (re: 4.4 grade point average) ought to be ashamed, though I expect he is not. I have seen gloating administrators brag that say, half a class is on the honor roll but that simply cannot be true, or, as they still say in the South: "That dog don't hunt." Grade inflation was engendered by teachers to make themselves look good, and, sure as hell is hot, it does not help the kids.

My wife, Catherine, and I have seen all sorts of bad behavior tolerated by teachers and police because hardly anyone wants to rock the boat. The students are running the show since those who used to be in charge 20 years ago have abdicated most of their responsibility. Thus, a profound and pervasive apathy reigns.

In this languorous process we have dismissed sociologist Eric Hoffer's trenchant admonition:

> "If a society is to preserve its stability and a degree of continuity, it must know to keep its adolescents from imposing their tastes, attitudes, values, and fantasies on everyday life."
>
> <u>Reflections</u> <u>on</u> <u>the</u> <u>Human</u> <u>Condition</u>
> (New York: Harper & Row, 1973, p. 29)

But, isn't that exactly what we have done, under the nose of the NEA, the ACLU and all the other, disreputable "experts"? Clearly, we have turned over our schools to the kids. Given my background at an old-fashioned, strict Catholic high school, and as the son of tough but loving parents, I never would have predicted that Hoffer's warning would have been so completely neglected.

I discovered that Hoffer quote in Diana West's prescient book: <u>The</u> <u>Death</u> <u>of</u> <u>the</u> <u>Grown</u> <u>Up:</u> <u>How</u> <u>American's</u> <u>Arrested</u> <u>Development</u> <u>is</u> <u>Bringing</u> <u>Down</u> <u>Western</u> <u>Civilization</u> (St. Martin's Press, New York; 2007). She basically says that in molly-coddling our kids, in asking them how they feel every 5 seconds, in abstaining from any real discipline; in making the word, "Obedience" essentially extinct, that we are making "desire factories" out of them whereby they will never grow up. She writes:

> "Chucking maturity for eternal youth may have created the culture of perpetual

adolescence, but it should now become apparent that this isn't the same thing as cultural longevity. The question is, what if it turns out that forever young is fatal?" (p. xiv)

Her book is required reading if one wants to understand the ongoing disaster that has happened both to our youth and to our schools.

So, confronted with all of these factors, realizing that our schools <u>for</u> <u>years</u> <u>now</u> have been failing, understanding that the teachers' unions are much of the problem, grasping, too, that the chickens have come home to roost (There's that word again. His sins have found him out; his actions have caught up with him. <u>Brewer's</u> p. 227), what then must we do (The question is from Luke 3:10)?

First, surprisingly, one must act like a farmer, like I once was. If I grew a poor crop of Chardonnay wine grapes one year, whether in quality or quantity, the following year I did <u>not</u> carry out the same cultural practices. Rather, I changed same come cultural practices, perhaps many of them. I maintained good and complete records so that the next year, the 3rd year, I could look back to see what tactics worked and why. Essentially, I did not wish to make the same mistake twice.

In schools, the past tactics have not worked, yet, like Jack in office, we persist in them! It was a plain mistake to give teenagers all sorts of rights, to abolish all forms of physical punishment, and to allow youths to have cell phones on campus, etc. Finally, it needs to be generally recognized that these drastic changes have not worked, and, therefore, that they ought to be immediately rescinded since every day we slip the further.

Moreover, let us examine why and how we (The ACLU, specifically) removed all mention of God from the classroom. Many forget that we used to teach religion all the time in public schools, that prayer used to start and end the day, that teachers used to say, "God is watching you" to discourage bad behavior. (Note the hammer!) Is it too much to ask for God's reinstatement in schools, to moderate behavior, and to set a better tone? We seem to have discarded the notion, as Dr. Thomas E Woods, Jr. writes that "Christianity was the most important factor shaping the colonists" (The Politically Incorrect Guide to American History Regnery Publishing, Inc; Washington DC; 2004, p.1) Is it not time to bring Him back? One must ask: How many of our problems with rampant bullying and hazing in schools only exist there because God has been banished from the classroom?

Obviously, I am a strong believer in Catholic education. I had 8 years with the nuns at American Martyrs (they always were kind and fair, despite the Church-hating myth that says otherwise), 4 years of the Augustinians at Villanova, and 2 years of the Jesuits at Gonzaga University, that is, before I went "off-track" to that archetypal hippie school, UC Santa Cruz where the mad mantra was "Do what you like", and "Whomever it hurts, let them be damned." The Catholic education taught me, on the other hand, that I was assuredly not the center of the universe, and, at the same time, that I must respect others. I was taught that I was infinitesimally small part of a larger community and inside that nation, whether we knew it or not, we were all linked. Recalling John Donne's parable:

> "No man is an Island, entire of itself;
> every man is a piece of the Continent, a
> part of the main . . ."

(Ernest Hemmingway used the last lines of the parable for the title of his novel: <u>For</u> <u>Whom</u> <u>the</u> <u>Bell</u> <u>Tolls</u>.) I maintain that Catholic schools, in the main, stress more the interdependency of man, and that public schools stress more the supremacy of the individual, which is the opposite.

I believe, too, that decreased levels of respect for others lead to bullying and hazing. If I do not think we are linked in my way, I am free (sic) to do whatever I want, that is, absent any other constraining rules. Students, many of them, do not think it is important to be kind to others. As a society, we must begin for the first time to ask ourselves: Why do they think so?

On this long sailing, may we tack back a tad further? Given:

1) unrespected authority
2) lowly discipline
3) lousy test scores
4) ridiculous spending

can it not be said that bullying and hazing is but a symptom of the longer issue: By any measure, our schools are failing, dying, like a ship full of holes about to founder. The proof: Bad behavior is not properly punished. Few teachers stick their necks out. Graduates (faux) are unprepared and undisciplined. Paralysis rules, despite vast sums of monies. Clarion calls for revived justice and action, like ours, are constantly ignored. Schools are often governed by the Peter Principle which says that people rise to the level of their incompetence, and, unfortunately, stay there. After reading Chapter Two perhaps you may agree with us that the higher level administrators are pretty much untouchable, protected by an unmoveable bureaucracy and NEA-engendered laws. For example, some of the NEA-written legislation passed in Albany for use in New York state is legally unrescindable. This is collusion at the highest level of the oligarchy in charge! Given New York's perilous financial state, the passing of such legislation (to guarantee pension plans down the road, and that they keep pace with inflation) was wildly irresponsible.

Yet, that is a moot point since soon New York State (and many others) will run out of money. It is only a question of when it will happen. My father used to warn me to watch out for the pensions. (I was 4 years old. I thought he had said "Watch out for the pigeons!," he worried that they might defecate on me. Ha!) No doubt exists that sometime soon pension checks will not be mailed since they cannot be covered.

Few seem too worried about all of this, at least nobody within the educational establishment; that is because there, selfishness is the governing force. It says: If I am happy, the world is happy." In other words, the egoist's chant. How else could all the stone throwers, Irish or otherwise, be so soundly rejected, so consistently ignored? We need to take poet Kenneth Patchen's words: "Sleepers Awake" to heart some day soon, to reform this growing mess, but in the meantime

1) we are losing the hearts and minds of kids
2) we are spending way too much money
3) bullying and hazing continue; indeed, with the ever expanding cyber world, it expands and grows, metastasizing like some rank cancer

or renegade tumor on the brain while those charged with stemming it snooze, nap, doze, while their mouths loll open, ready to catch flies.

Am I too harsh? I must ask myself this question all the time since lives are at stake. I believe Mrs. Ostrich and Penguin should be moved to another position, <u>not</u> fired, as I sometimes wrote to the inactive, titular heads, since they have shown neither the ability nor inclination to completely eliminate bullying and hazing. Maybe they wish it to go away but do not know how to make it happen. (I will speak to that later.) This result is a judicious one.

As much as one might like to comply with educators who say that all is hunky-dory, super-dooper, copasetic, at the schools, the preponderant statistical weight says exactly the opposite. Despite decades of above-inflation rate spending, more rules and staff and guidelines than ever before, more in-house, upgrading training, more teacher conferences led by presumed experts, and a larger supporting bureaucracy than history has ever seen, the simple fact is that the test scores are flat and graduates not ready for the world.

And what a world! Asian countries, in particular, are passing us by, especially with regards to math and sciences, as if we were standing still. Our bicycle's chain has slipped off the main front sprocket, which means that, no matter how hard we pedal, we do not move. The educational system, we hope we have demonstrated to you, is

    1) bloated
    2) corrupt
    3) unmoving

4) too expensive and, most importantly

5) absolutely unable to reform itself.

And that tells us, therefore, that anyone "in the inside" still praising it after all this swollen spending, has an ulterior motive which would be "to feather his nest," which <u>Brewer's</u> defines as:

To provide for one's own interest, especially financial. The phrase is commonly used with implications of disapproval. (P. 419)

You can say that again, 'eavesdropper' (one who stations himself in the eaves-drip to overhear what was said in the house)!:

> "Under our tents I'll play the eavesdropper
> To hear if any mean to shrink from me"
>> Shakespeare, Richard III (V, iii, 221)

How I would like to be an eavesdropper, one with the sharpest hearing, at their meetings of apologia! As educators continue to shrink away from this fray or battle, perhaps playing the eavesdropper on each other (inventing a new treachery as yet unseen) feathering <u>their</u> nests to the point of <u>our</u> insolvency, our schools slip the more, only slip. Those in charge do not want to stir up any trouble by intimating that we might be in a teeny bit of trouble. This is a con game, of course. They try to con us, and what is more, in defending the mess that is our schools to each other, they are conning each other.

Recall the film Apollo 13. In it, after the fuel tanks had just been stirred, Commander Jim Lovell, played in the film by Tom Hanks, says, clearly: "Houston, We have a problem." He did not try to deny it; rather, he knew they had to <u>act</u>. Later, the stubborn Kranz fellow, played by Ed Harris, says that we must "work the problem," and avoid all internecine squabbling. In charge of the efforts to save the dying spaceship and its crew as it loses it oxygen and fuel (sound familiar?), Kranz says, famously:

"Failure is not an option."

Today, we need his Extreme Determination (note the appropriate acronym to match his name), but, I wonder: Can we muster it?[3]

So, unrecognized, unattacked, the problem of bullying and hazing grows, expands, multiplies. Since educational standards are so lax, since students are routinely passed on when they should be held back, since so many teachers, compelled by "No Child left Behind," routinely teach only for a test, most schools have become mediocre or worse. But, again, you ask: My proof?

For 2 years, 4 terms, over 14 courses, teaching English to roughly 400 students at a local college, I saw first-hand the starkest decline: Not that the student were unintelligent, no, but, that the majority of them lacked two things:

    1) Basic knowledge, and

---

[3]   Comments, taken from Imagine Entertainments <u>Apollo 13</u>, directed by Ron Howard, written by William Broyles, Jr. and Al Reinart, 2005.

2) Essential skills, which in turn, had to have been caused by two factors:
   a) A high school which had short-changed them, and
   b) Their own laziness

(The percentage of a to b is a "chicken or an egg" discussion, one profitless but best settled at a Dutch bargain, that is, one settled over drinks, the Dutch being formerly reputed to be steady drinkers. Brewer's, p. 367)

Grasp this: These students who had graduated from high school, mostly 18 years old or thereabouts, when I told them that I was a Truman baby, they asked me:

"Does that mean you never tell a fib?"

Further, many did not know who JFK or RFK were, had not heard of the Vietnam War, and were not familiar with Dr. King's "I have a dream" speech. And on and on, without end. How could this be? Nearly every evening I would repeat back to my wife at dinner some new, startling gap.

While a freshman at Gonzaga I took my first English class, Principles of Exposition, from an elderly Jesuit. Nearly every day he read to us from Winston Churchill, praising his diction and pace, phraseology and style. He told us about how Churchill went toe-to-toe with the passive Prime Minister, Stephen Baldwin, who at that time, the late 1930s, did not much fear or fret over emerging Hitler. With words, Churchill had helped to awaken a sleeping nation, and, of course, in the process he saved his country from the Hun.

So, it was natural for me to turn to Churchill for my own students (since I was teaching essentially the same class); yet, when I did, I was aghast to find out that most of the students had barely heard of him. How could it be that the seminal Englishman of the last century could have been so quickly forgotten? What does that gap of knowledge say about any purported shared history? Indeed, what does it say about our schools? Are the teachers asleep? Is it not further proof that our culture is either lost or has altered to some new and aberrant and unknowable form?

To return to my students for a moment, many could not write the cursive form decently at all; so strong is the dedication to the computer that penmanship is becoming a lost art. Many could not spell well, since a reliance on Spellcheck predominates. Sometimes I would argue with a student on this point: That one needs to spell well, and that Spellcheck is intrinsically unreliable; yet, I always felt afterwards that I had lost soundly the debate and that most of the students thought me to be an

1) old-fogey
2) a dinosaur
3) a Luddite
4) a throwback, or
5) a pious humbug, take one's pick.

Many of the students, either from laziness or inept high school teaching, or perhaps from a combination of both, could not write one error-free, proper sentence, and you may forget about long or complicated paragraphs, rising action, pathos, denouement, essays, satire, proving claims, and pretty much everything else. Many did not know much about story or character development, nor did they wish to. By and large, they do not read. And, thus, the ability to write well is fast disappearing, period, if you may excuse the pun.

My kindly and astute office mate, a Statistics and Math teacher, said to me that the same sort of diminution of knowledge and skills is taking place in his field as well. As a math teacher he described it to me as a rate of change, or delta. He said to me (and here I paraphrase) that students' abilities are declining at a rate so quick that we cannot know how bad things are until they will have gotten much worse. Is this the very best that we can do?

As a side issue, another salient question needs to be asked: Has the quality of public sector employees, including educators, gone down in the last 20 years? Do superintendents demand excellence as they ought to? As they used to? The possibility that they do not should be considered and redressed. It is a natural part of human nature to become lazy over time, especially when the job is virtually guaranteed, the health benefits is very generous and the pension plan is deemed rock-solid. Absent a meritocracy, how does an educational leader insist upon the very best? Pretty difficult, considering the circumstances. How does one fire a teacher who is simply not doing his job? The NEA has things so tightly wired now that any change, for good or for bad, is hard to accomplish.

To step back and make a separate ascension, as we ply our small boat for the finish, I will make the point that ever since "People" magazine was first published, our nation's people no longer really believe in education; rather, we revere its opposite, entertainment: That is our god, our new god. Witness the escapist movies, rap scum, the mindless reality shows, the driveling and inane news which is actually celebrity gossip. Bit by bit, whit by whit, dot by dot, we are losing the ability to think, to gather to oneself wit and calibration; and the unchecked bullying and the hazing that flourishes at so many local schools is but a small, yet vibrant symptom of that larger, growing cancer. I hope that I have convinced the reader that many of our schools have become perhaps irredeemably infected with this brought-upon-ourselves disease of lassitude.

At base, how did this happen (and thence I shall deport for a deep glass of my favorite Terran and some slices of my very best salsiccia cinghiale, and gladly so since, as Will writes, "Good wine is a good familiar creature if it be used well." (Othello, II, 3, 315)? Easy, now, easy. Back in the 60s, after the two Kennedy brothers and Dr. Martin King Jr., all three decent men and, by the way, properly taught, had been assassinated, we Americans went quite wild (Are we still, Ollie? Are we?) Here is a partial list of our still unacknowledged mistakes:

1) Promiscuity: Let's change partners as often as we can!
2) Drugs: Why not? I know that they are safe.
3) Rejection of all authority: To the cop: Screw you.
4) Anti-patriotism: Vietnam, a debacle. 'Nuff said.
5) Victimhood: Blame someone else for your mistake. Pansyhood.
6) Selfishness: Ego's run, unabated.

I list six since that number is so noddy close to sex, which, looking backwards, mushroomed or take-turns sprouted, has probably hatched half our later problems. But, whoever wants to look down the road a tingle? We have became so quickly lost, rebels without a cause, pushed about by varying, indeed, conflicting desires. We began to believe in little save our own private happiness or pleasure or contentment, call it what you will, and in that rut of darkest passage we have begun to lose our culture, our society. The bullying and hazing is just an indicator.

For, what binds us together? We must look to item #6: If we do not care for the other, we easily can say: "I can do whatever I want." Selfishness is most insidious since it creeps in slowly, under the door, like the unbeatable plague in Albert Camus' book of the same name. Suddenly, or so it seems, it is in the room, outside, everywhere. Is this not what has happened to America?

"I can do whatever I want," that foolish mantra of the 60s, stands like a drunken soldier, next to my earlier comment from the egoist:

"If I am happy, the world is happy."

Selfishness says to all bankers:

"If you can get away with it, go ahead."

(Guess what? They did, and still are.) People from my parents' generation, on the other hand, used to ask themselves:

"Is it right? Is it proper?"

Now, we are more likely to say:

"Will I get caught?"

because, just as St. Joseph lost his hammer at the high school, we Americans have misplaced our individual and collective moral compasses. A compass: What is that? Which is to say, not to put too fine a point on it: Our society, in not stopping bullying and hazing, and with its ever coarsening amusements, is slowly and imperceptibly losing its soul. The fat is in the fire. Something has been let out inadvertently which will cause a "regular flare up." (Brewer's, p. 415)

So, with Luke at my side, I ask again, but, this time, the more beseechingly:

"What then must we do?" (3:10)

To answer I will start at any school and then, later, move outward towards a greater thunder. Many things to do, all ye rapt scavengers, there are so many things to do:

1) In schools, ban all cell phones. They, in school, have no place. Unless we do this thoroughly we are as doomed as prideful Lucifer. They are distracting; and a detriment and hindrance to learning. Like much of technology they inhibit focus which is essential for learning. Indeed, as technology morphs to multiple forms as yet unseen, I wonder if we, increasingly passive and distracted, may lose our ability to:

    a) follow an order

    b) complete a task

    c) simply concentrate on and finish the job at hand.

I fear cell phones will continue their inevitable mercantile march to some mermaid form unable to be controlled.

Akin to the overly elaborate medical field, phone technology, at least in schools, is way ahead of teachers' ability to control it. Why did we ever let this kids have them? Because we were weak and slow, like some 3rd sailor who can no longer reach the shot down the line.

2) Bring back, please, some judicious corporal punishment. Teachers should be able, <u>if</u> <u>all</u> <u>other</u> <u>methods</u> <u>have</u> <u>failed</u>, to threaten, instill fear, and intimidate. Why not? As I wrote in Chapter One; "Raven," at my high school, if I screwed up, I got punished. Refind St. Joseph's now-lost hammer, in other words. Again, the Latin: <u>In</u> <u>loco</u> <u>parentis</u>. In place of a parent.

3) Make <u>unlevel</u> the playing field. Give back to teachers, and seriously so, the steady obligation to discipline, not just to go through the motions, which is what we see today. Regain authority and if a student does not show respect for a teacher's authority, suspension or expulsion is next. Students are <u>not</u> equal to teachers in power, or brains, since they are in their adolescent nonage.

4) Bring back many other things from the past. Since schools are now paid based on attendance, they are not inclined to suspend or expel students. Stop this <u>pro</u> <u>rata</u> scheme. To combat the growing truancy problem, bring back truant

officers who, back in my long distant youth, wore policeman-style caps, badges, and guns; they actually took kids to juvenile hall if they missed class: What a concept! Most fundamentally, throughout, bring back the idea of obedience.

5) Immediately abolish all study halls, extra aides, filler classes, most conference days (there are far too many), all Advanced Placement classes (AP) which are only possible now due to that greatest of sins, grade inflation. Most of these things require too much money and we are going broke, in case nobody has noticed. Flunk a child if he has not, nearly, mastered a class since to pass him on, which continually happens now, does to him no favors. In short, grade inflation equals a fake education.

6) Merit pay for teachers. Not surprisingly, their unions have fought it assiduously for decades. Such an obvious idea it is, one quite common in the business world where incentives are everywhere, but, big surprise, the NEA, perhaps the most powerful union in the country, (It, along with the trial lawyers' association helped to elect our very poor and sexually distracted president, Bill Clinton) fights against that needed reform. Its equivalent would have been

accomplished in the business world in a matter of days.

7) Fire, or move aside, administrators, like Mrs. Ostrich and Penguin who do not possess the gumption or intestinal strength or impassioned temper to eliminate completely the bullying and hazing problem. No more sweeping the dust under the rug, and no more obfuscation or evasions.

8) Stop funding schools from property tax, and rescind unfunded state mandates: An oligarchy's collusion. Instead, fund schools from any state's general fund. Climbing property taxes are killing the idea of home ownership and encouraging the exodus from all property tax offending states. Example: New York.

Now, eight is a fine place to stop since 1) I feel my heart beating at an ascending and scary rate, and, 2) unless we make these moves, and soon, we will be completely "behind the eight ball," that is stuck "in a dangerous position from which it is impossible to escape." (Brewer's, p. 381)

Moving to a vaster scale, hearing a few ominous thunderclaps far in the distance sailing south, just beyond Zeus and Neptune, Ariadne and Helena, we ought to

1) Renounce corrupting moral relativism which says (from Woodstock on down for these last 40 years) shot I can do whatever I want, and whenever I want. It celebrates impulse release

and unfettered desire, which can easily become slavish. Read the Greeks and what they said about Moderation. This is not new. Follow the commandments which are meant to protect us from our false or baser natures. Do not hate anyone since it only brings unhappiness. Bring God back to the classroom.

2) Seek to guide, firmly and lovingly, teenagers since, simply, expectedly, they need it. Their brains and emotions are still unformed and unfinished. Stop treating them like adults, since that tactic was but a snare and a delusion. (Brewer's, p. 323) Be stern when mistakes are made and strongly congratulatory when success is achieved. Seek to limit teenagers' use of the phrase "I want" since that is not how and why the world works. Unless we bring back a much stronger discipline to the schools, a real discipline, we will have raised an enter generation that cannot follow orders and, that is a frightening thought for society. Think for a moment of the larger implications of millions of students that cannot take and carry out a command.

3) Get rid of this victimhood or pansiate idea, promoted by many teachers, that the world owes me a living. Encourage the opposite: Self-reliance and goal setting. Find good friends and be a reliable friend to them, asking for

nothing in return (Re: Seneca). Avoid (that beautiful word, _Evitare_, in Italian) all those with bad habits or unkindness, attached to their natures, like one would shun wild dogs or the plague.

4) Speaking of illnesses, avoid all mendacious, prevarications, fibs, and connivings. Tell the whole truth and nothing but the truth. Convey no false images. It is common now to lie. The dog asks the cat: How did all this start?

Instead, practice the Hebrew concept of _Dugri_, or a man's utmost honesty. That way, too, you won't have to keep your lies straight. Thank you, again, Sister Saint Anne. Get rid of the baloney in the educational world, all the phony populism and empty cant. Use clear, concise language to address this big problem, not fuzzy modulations. Avoid most uses of the conditional tense: "We could . . ." since they lead nowhere. As a problem grows more complex, ratchet up the language's rigor.

Watching the movie _Bullitt_ last night, I saw this important difference in the tone or diction. Frank Bullitt says, plainly: "Seal it, Barney!" Whereas the evil and ineffectual Mr. Chalmers says, "It would be a good idea if we were to . . ." Who got the most done? Frank Bullitt speaks in a different manner: Clear, concise, unambiguous, a word-form to which we must return (Bullitt, screenplay by Alan R. Trustman and Harry Kleiner, Directed by Peter Yates, Warner Brothers and Solar Production, 1968).

5) Recognize a problem and attack it unremittingly. Do not give up! The harder the issue, the more complete and thorough must be one's resolve. This is where the inability or unwillingness of school officials to attack bullying and hazing is so discouraging. They could solve this bullying and hazing thing, for example, but they do not, apparently, want to. As Col. Ralph Peters says, "If we do not have the courage to fire people, nothing changes." (Fox News, January 10, 2010). Expand determination at one's core.

Five is a good place to pause, not to stop, it being the sum of 2 and 3, the first even and first odd compound. We have the Five nations, the Five Senses, and, yes, the Five Wits . . .

* * *

By now, sailors we are near done. Work beckons to all of us, saying clearly aloud: "Bring back. Bring back." And with the naval chaplain at Pearl Harbor during the attack we hear: "Praise the Lord and pass the ammunition." (Brewer's, p. 888) 'Tis apt, since our schools are under attack, or at war, but mostly from within.

May one ask: Is there not, again, a place in the sun wherein this grimmer life of ours today may thankfully depart? Can we not find again, a decent and less caustic place? Our weaker children are at stake and are now in danger. We must protest them from all oblivion.

Today, many sailors warn the captain that the ship is swamped, but they are not heard. All of that and more is forgotten. Can we not admit, at last, that so many things done in education in the last 40 years were mistakes, just as it was a mistake for the US Army to sit on its rear 70 miles west of Berlin in April 1945 while the Russians took that city and its treasures, pillaging, raping, burning, looting.

Today, I can see my father, fresh from heaven, glaring, glowering, and his naval voice bellows to me:

"Do not forget, remember!"

And:

"We must refuse to accept anything less than excellence!"

He is fierce in his reminding, and always gives short, imperial commands. And, why not? He taught to me how to follow an order. A lost skill, fellow bosuns? Lost? Though much remains to capture the elusive flame of a better life.

That is because, it must be thought, and it must be again taught, that tangling evil exists in this eroded and broken world. Bullying and hazing is but one expression of that evil, and, as it grows and spreads and expands, as it is tolerated and ignored (as our family has seen), it reflects even more the calmest evil. When school officials look the other way, pretending to avoid its existence, or when they are, as documented here, namby-pamby in attacking it (wishy-washy, or molly-coddling will also do), when they, stepping backwards, defer from vanquishing it (Yes. Let us use that good Latin word derived from <u>Vincere</u>: to conquer), they demonstrate to all an even greater and expanding evil.

Prefiguring St. Augustine, let us no longer act as if evil does not exist in this world. It does. Bullying and hazing is a terrible evil. Let us, then, turning to excoriate the other side of the dialectic, banish moral relativism which dictates that all actions are equal. It is like a bad weed which must be pulled out of the ground by its whole root. In schools its promulgation has made a recent non-order which simply does not work. Our society, our culture, our schools are near to suicide; they do not work, and are broken. Let us no longer fool ourselves that they do. All of this is our choice, a choice to avert any further decline, and to embrace older standards of morality which once worked pretty well.

Know, please, that history will measure us and curse all our inaction. Again, consider, please, that frail children (though they act not the part) are at stake and are now in grave danger or harm's way.

So, I see St. Joseph, that good man with the callused hands; he is a friend, a carpenter. He says, "The hammer please." I see his smile, his eyes keen and eager, and hear him for the first time say to all those gathered here to listen:

"Let us have no more sloppiness in my shop! Do you hear me? And that's that!"